ISRAEL

POCKET GUIDE

 **Walking Eye**
mobile app

Discover the world's best destinations with the Insight Guides Walking Eye app, available to download for free in the App Store and Google Play.

The container app provides easy access to fantastic free content on events and activities taking place in your current location or chosen destination, with the possibility of booking, as well as the regularly-updated Insight Guides travel blog: Inspire Me. In addition, you can purchase curated, premium destination guides through the app, which feature local highlights, hotel, bar, restaurant and shopping listings, an A to Z of practical information and more. Or purchase and download Insight Guides eBooks straight to your device.

TOP 10 ATTRACTIONS

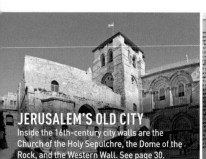

JERUSALEM'S OLD CITY
Inside the 16th-century city walls are the Church of the Holy Sepulchre, the Dome of the Rock, and the Western Wall. See page 30.

DEAD SEA SCROLLS
On display at the Israel Museum are the Dead Sea Scrolls – the oldest known version of the Old Testament. See page 44.

SEA OF GALILEE
Despite its name, the Sea of Galilee is in fact a lake, surrounded by a halo of mountains, overlooked from its shores by towns and holy places. See page 62.

RED SEA MARINE LIFE
Incredible marine life and coral formations make the Red Sea, the closest tropical waters to Europe, a diver's paradise. See page 82.

FLOATING IN THE DEAD SEA
At 405 meters (1,300ft) below sea level, the Dead Sea is the lowest accessible place on earth, with an excessive salt content that enables bathers to float. See page 78.

TEL AVIV SEAFRONT
Lined with cafés, bars, and restaurants, this is a great place to take the city in. See page 47.

JAFFA (YAFO)
Where it all began: it is said Noah settled here after the Great Flood. See page 49.

BAHÁ'Í HILLSIDE GARDENS, HAIFA
The world's longest hillside gardens are to be found in Haifa at the headquarters of the Bahá'í religion. See page 71.

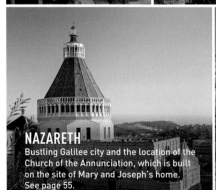

NAZARETH
Bustling Galilee city and the location of the Church of the Annunciation, which is built on the site of Mary and Joseph's home. See page 55.

BETHLEHEM
A picturesque Palestinian hilltop town overlooking the Judean Desert, known as the birthplace of Christ, 9km (6 miles) from Jersualem. See page 45.

A PERFECT DAY

7:00am

Early morning dip
Take a quick dip in the Mediterranean while the sun is still benign at one of Tel Aviv's beaches. Mezizim beach, near Tel Aviv port, is one of the best, or wherever is the nearest beach to your hotel.

10.00am

All aboard
Board the recently opened Tel Aviv–Jerusalem fast rail link at Haganah Station for the 30-minute ride to Jerusalem. At Jerusalem station switch to the light rail and travel along Jaffa Road to the Old City.

11:00am

Explore the Old City
Enter the Old City through the Jaffa Gate and walk through the Muslim quarter market down to the Temple Mount where you can see the exquisite Dome of the Rock and the nearby El Aqsa Mosque. Back out to the Western Wall, the only remaining edifice from the Second Temple.

12:30pm

Lunch on Via Dolorosa
Make your way to the Lions Gate and start strolling along the Via Dolorosa. Have a light classic hummus and pita lunch at Abu Shukri where the Via Dolorosa turns into Al Wadi Street.

9.00am

Prepare for Jerusalem
Cover up for the trip to Jerusalem to see the holy sites both out of modesty, and to protect yourself from the sun. Take a taxi to Haganah Station.

8:00am

Breakfast
Enjoy a classic Israeli breakfast at Café Nimrod in Tel Aviv Port or back at your hotel.

IN **ISRAEL**

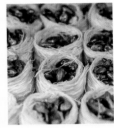

3:00pm

Along Jaffa Road
Back out of the Jaffa Gate and stroll along Jaffa Road through Zion Square towards Mahanei Yehuda market. Take the light rail if you don't have the time or energy.

4:30pm

Mahnei Yehuda market
Take in the energy and buzz at Mahnei Yehuda market. Have some freshly squeezed juice, tea or coffee and try some baklava desert pastry. It's a 15-minute walk from here to the station, then board the train back to Tel Aviv.

8:30pm

Dinner in Jaffa Port
After freshening up at the hotel head for Jaffa Port and try one of the restaurants there like the Old Man and the Sea for a traditional Middle Eastern meal. By 10.30pm, Tel Aviv's famous night life is just getting started. Try Teder FM at 9 Derekh Jaffa or Levontin 7 (that's also the address). If bars aren't your thing, just stroll along the seafront promenade and enjoy the bustling night life in the city that never stops.

2:00pm

The Holy Sepulchre
Reach the Church of the Holy Sepulchre at the end of the Via Dolorosa.

CONTENTS

INTRODUCTION

Israel confounds expectations. It is a nation rooted in religion, yet the majority of Israel's Jewish population are brazenly secular, turning to religion for births, bar and bat mitzvahs, weddings, and funerals, but preferring to spend their Sabbaths and holidays on the beach or in cafés rather than in formal prayer.

There are picturesque bastions of orthodoxy in Jerusalem and elsewhere that are a quaint mixture of medieval Poland and the Middle East, but outside these locations, long rabbinical beards are rare, many restaurants serve forbidden unkosher foods, and women dress anything but modestly.

Israel is similar in size to New Jersey or Wales but has far more geographical and demographical diversity. Few locations offer as much per-square-kilometer to sustain the spirit, feed the intellect, and stimulate the senses. It is a place where three continents – Africa, Asia, and Europe – all meet, and the landscape and the people are a fusion of these three continents.

You don't have to be a believer to savour all this. The miracles may be a matter of personal faith, but what can't be disputed historically is that this is the land of the Bible, the cradle of monotheism, a geography familiar from

Four Seas

This is a land of four seas: the Mediterranean, the tropical Red Sea with its remarkable marine life, the Sea of Galilee where Jesus is believed to have walked on water, and the Dead Sea, the lowest point on earth where the excessive salt allows bathers to effortlessly float on its surface.

Café culture, Tel Aviv

childhood religious instruction. The names resonate in visitors' minds and stimulate their curiosity: Jerusalem, the Galilee, Bethlehem, Nazareth, Jaffa, Jericho, and the River Jordan.

In Jerusalem, you can pray at the one remaining wall of the Temple that the Romans left intact; you can walk along the Via Dolorosa to the Church of the Holy Sepulchre; you can see the El-Aqsa Mosque on the Temple Mount where the Prophet Mohammed came to pray during his lifetime and the adjacent Dome of the Rock, one of the world's most exquisite buildings.

ABUZZ WITH ENERGY

While Israel's identity was forged in the past, Israelis, at least outside of Jerusalem, live unashamedly in the present. Tel Aviv epitomizes 21st-century Israel. The city that reputedly never stops buzzes with an abundance of energy, creativity, and innovation from its golden Mediterranean beaches to Bauhaus architecture and gleaming office towers that contain its famous high-tech start-ups and many restaurants, cafés, bars and nightclubs in between. Haifa has its beaches and nightlife too, as well as the stunning gardens of the Bahá'í temple on the Mount Carmel hillside. Elsewhere there are the remains of the former Roman capital of Caesarea, the Crusader port of Akko, the hot baths of Tiberias, and the hilltop mystical town of Safed and much more.

The rolling green hills of the Galilee and Golan, and the empty stretches and open blue skies of the Arava and Negev Deserts aside, this is one of the world's most densely packed pieces of real estate. Israel's population is more than 9 million, while 5 million Palestinians live in the adjoining Gaza Strip and West Bank.

For many visitors, the enduring attraction of Israel is its people – the inheritors of the rich tapestry of many invading cultures that have woven their history into the region. Contrary to perceived stereotypes, most Israelis are neither right-wing religious zealots nor left-wing peace activists. Most are middle of the road and more concerned about the performance of Tel Aviv's stock market, their favourite

Bahá'í Hillside Gardens, Haifa

football team or the Israel Philharmonic Orchestra. One attribute shared by all Israelis, whether they are religious or secular, of European or Afro/Asian origin, right-wing or left-wing, Jewish or Muslim, is a desire to talk to strangers. In chatting to tourists, Israelis may simply be wanting to practice their English, vent their anger at Israel's perceived misrepresentation in the international media, promote the Palestinian cause or, perhaps sell something or spend time with a good-looking visitor. Whatever the motivation, Israelis are undeniably friendly.

The Promised Land

Sea and sunshine aside, this is the Promised Land to which, it is said, Moses led the Children of Israel. It is where Abraham made his covenant with God, Christ preached his sermons, and Mohammed ascended to heaven.

Israelis consider themselves to be part of Europe, although the country, via Egypt's Sinai Peninsula, forms the only continental land bridge between Asia and Africa. The European illusion is maintained in the spruce streets of Tel Aviv and Haifa, while because of Israel's geopolitical isolation from the Arab world, the country is permitted to be an associate member of the European Union and a full member of most European institutions, including the UEFA football federation and Eurovision.

However, from the narrow alleyways and markets of Jerusalem's Old City to the stunning desert landscapes, it is clear that the cultural and physical landscape of Israel is not European. Nor is the climate, which is hot and dry in the summer and mild and wet in the winter with no rain between April and October. The geographical diversity brings itself

Hikers in the the Negev Desert

to bear on the weather: the Mediterranean coast is humid, while Jerusalem, at 800 meters (2,625ft) above sea level, has cool summer evenings and cold winters. Nearby Eilat, in the south on the Red Sea, is warm in the winter and scorching in the summer.

THE MISSING PEACE

Of course, the major blot on the landscape is the failure of Israelis and Palestinians to reach a lasting peace. In recent decades the search for peace has proved elusive as the country drifts to the right, with religious fundamentalism and nationalism taking a firmer hold on events. Even so, visitors who engage in more extended conversation with Jews and Muslims will be surprised to discover how much desire there is toward reaching a compromise, even if it is only because of a lack of stomach for the violent alternative.

Despite the challenges of the Israel-Palestinian conflict, Israel remains a vibrant democracy. The democratically elected politicians remain the undisputed masters of the army generals who have formed the nation's values. Although the Israeli military has a peerless reputation for executing the swift, the precise and the dramatically unexpected, the ubiquitous Israeli soldier, M16 slung casually over shoulder, appears slovenly and unregimented.

Israel's greatest achievements, however, have not been on the battlefield. This nation has been created out of immigrants from 80 countries, who shared a religious heritage and a desire to return to their ancestral homeland, but little else – not even a language. In the street you will hear an astonishing variety of languages: Russian, English, Arabic, Amharic,

Souk in Jerusalem's Old City

Relaxing in Eilat

Hungarian, French, Persian, Spanish, and Yiddish. Hebrew, the language of the Bible, has been resurrected and adapted to everyday life. The country has a 23% Arab minority and many small communities such as the Druze and Circassians, as well as hundreds of thousands of migrant workers, refugees, and long-stay tourists.

The garrulousness and infectious energy of its people ensure that Israel is seldom boring. The hedonistic visitor seeking sunshine, golden beaches, and nightlife, the nature lover in search of desert vistas and unique flora and fauna, and the historically curious seeking remains from biblical, Roman, or Crusader times will not be disappointed.

Most of all, religious visitors will usually come away with their beliefs reinforced, while non-believers have been known to return home with glimmerings of faith they didn't have when they set out on their journey.

A BRIEF HISTORY

Archeological evidence suggests that farming evolved in this region some 12,000 years ago and there are remains of human settlements on the Mediterranean coast, Judean Desert, and Jordan Valley. Canaanite city kingdoms developed in the heart of the "fertile crescent," along trading routes between the two regional powers – Egypt and Mesopotamia.

THE BIBLICAL PERIOD

The Book of Genesis tells us that Abraham moved from Mesopotamia in about 2000 BC, settling in Be'er Sheva and eventually buried in Hebron, which remains fiercely disputed until today by the descendants of his sons, Ishmael and Isaac. Abraham's Jewish descendants became known as the Israelites; according to Bible, after migrating to Egypt and living as slaves, they conquered Canaan in the story of Exodus, after being led through the desert by Moses. His successor Joshua led them into Canaan, winning the battle of Jericho, and establishing the Israelite capital in Hebron.

About 1000 BC, King David moved his capital from Hebron to a new city, which he built on a mountain top above a spring 29km (18 miles) to the north. He called it Jerusalem. His son King Solomon built the First Temple, which was destroyed by the Babylonians three centuries later. After a 40-year exile, the Jews returned to Jerusalem and rebuilt the Temple.

The ascendancy of the Fertile Crescent waned as the farming techniques developed in the region mimicked those in Europe, where cultivation was facilitated by a moister climate. The Jews, having split into the kingdoms of Israel and Judea were conquered first by the Greeks (although the Hasmonean dynasty recaptured the country for more than a century for the Jews in between), before the Romans arrived in 63 BC, renaming the region Palestine. In 37 BC, Herod, the Roman's client king of Judea, assumed the throne. Taking advantage of the prosperity that the Romans brought, he established his capital in Caesarea, rebuilt the Second Temple, and established lavish fortress palaces such as Masada overlooking the Dead Sea.

THE CHRISTIAN AND MUSLIM ERAS

A Galilean preacher named Jesus Christ tapped into some of the unrest created by the Roman occupation and the Jewish establishment led by Herod. In the AD 12, he was crucified in Jerusalem. His teachings slowly spread, with Armenia and Ethiopia among the first countries to adopt Christianity. However, it was not until AD 325 when Emperor Constantine of the Byzantine Eastern Roman Empire converted to Christianity that Palestine became recognized as the Holy Land. His mother Helena came and identified the sacred sites in Jerusalem, Bethlehem, Nazareth, and the Galilee, which are revered by the Orthodox and Catholic churches to this day.

Meanwhile, the Jews staged failed revolts against the Romans, resulting in the destruction of the Second Temple (only a western support wall was left standing) and after 132, were exiled. Jerusalem was renamed Aelia Capitolina. Many Jewish zealots held out at Herod's former Masada fortress before committing suicide rather than being taken captive.

Jerusalem remained Christian until the Muslim conquest in 637. The Muslims renamed the Temple Mount Haram esh-Sharif (Noble Sanctuary) and the El Aqsa Mosque where Mohammed had prayed during his lifetime was enlarged. The Dome of the Rock was built in 691 as a shrine where it is believed Mohammed ascended to heaven from.

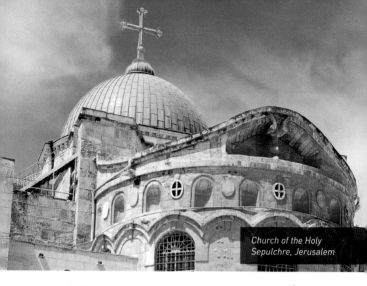

Church of the Holy Sepulchre, Jerusalem

In 1099, the Crusaders conquered Jerusalem, converting the Dome of the Rock into a church and the El Aqsa Mosque into a royal palace. The Church of the Holy Sepulchre, identified by Helena as the site of the crucifixion but destroyed by the Fatimid Muslims in 1009, was rebuilt in 1149.

In the 13th century the Mamelukes, Muslim slaves that became knights, seized Egypt and much of the Levant and drove the Crusaders out of Palestine. The Crusaders lost their last foothold in Akko in 1291. The Mamelukes, who left little beyond an architectural heritage, were defeated by the Ottoman Turks in 1516, whose ruler Suleiman Magnificent completed the walls around Jerusalem (today's Old City walls) in 1541.

By the 19th century, despite eventually repelling Napoleon's invasion, the Ottoman Empire was in decline and the European powers began staking a claim in Palestine through churches,

monasteries and other religious institutions in Jerusalem and the rest of the country. The Russians built on the land to the west of Jerusalem's Old City, the Germans built the tallest church in Jerusalem and the French built sprawling monasteries in and around Jerusalem and the Galilee. The British eventually captured Palestine from the Ottomans in 1917 during the First World War, and were given a mandate to rule by the League of Nations.

THE VICTORY OF ZIONISM

The British issued the Balfour Declaration on November 2 1917, which favoured the establishment of a homeland for the Jewish people in Palestine. Since the exile of the Israelites, the Jews had yearned to return to Zion (Mount Zion is one of the hills of the Old City). However, the conventional religious assumption was that the return to Zion would take place only when the Messiah would come. Even so, some small religious communities had remained in Jerusalem, as well as Tiberias and Safed in the Galilee. Many Jews, including the revered 12th-century Jewish philosopher Maimonides, had returned to Palestine over the centuries. However, it was secular rather than religious Jews that led the return to Zion.

In the 19th century growing antisemitism in Europe resulted in the rise of political Zionism. After the assassination of Tsar Alexander in 1881, antisemitism reached fever pitch in the Russian Empire and hundreds of Jews were slaughtered in government-sponsored pogroms. Millions emigrated to Western Europe and the US, but a small number were drawn to Palestine and founded farming villages with names like Rishon Lezion (first to Zion) and Petah Tikvah (opening of hope).

With the rise of nationalism, the Yiddish-speaking Jews of the region, many of whom questioned their religious heritage, began to look for an identity. It came from Central Europe after Theodor Herzl, a Hungarian Jew working as a journalist covering the trial of French officer Lt. Col. Alfred Dreyfus, falsely accused and found guilty of spying for the Germans, only because he was Jewish, despaired of the plight of Jews in Europe. He established the Zionist Congress in 1897 and the political infrastructure of a future state was put in place.

Most of the early Jewish immigrants were socialists who set up collectively owned farms, kibbutz. Degania, which was the first kibbutz, was established in 1909 and followed in 1921 by Nahalal, the first *moshav* (agricultural cooperative). The Haganah Jewish paramilitary organization founded in 1920 was the forerunner of the Israeli army and the Histadrut trade union movement founded the same year shaped the economy. The farmer-soldiers of the kibbutzim and *moshavim* set the future borders of Israel.

Front page of The Palestine Post, May 18, 1948

Not all Jews were socialists. Many were capitalists and in 1909 some founded a garden city north of Jaffa called Tel Aviv. Others were revisionists led by Zeev Jabotinsky who had a maximalist vision of a future state and a more militant military doctrine in how to achieve it. But it was the more pragmatic socialist David Ben Gurion who became the leader of the Zionists.

ARAB RESISTANCE

In the 19th century Palestinian Arabs initially welcomed Jewish immigrants. Their numbers were small and they boosted the region's economy. If the Balfour Declaration was a victory for Zionist diplomacy, it was wake-up call to the Arab World. Arab rioting and violent conflict between Jews and Arab spread as the British quickly came to regret the Balfour Declaration. The large desert area east of the Jordan River was split off from

Palestine in 1922 and named Jordan under the Hashemite dynasty, a tribe from Hejaz to the south.

Events in Europe were about to impact the region as the Nazis took power in Germany in 1933 and the continent began its dark descent towards the Holocaust. In 1931, there were 175,000 Jews in Palestine and as Jews fled Germany that number doubled by 1936 to 385,000. Under Arab pressure, the British restricted Jewish emigration to Palestine, blocking escape for the European Jewry, 6 million of whom were murdered in the Holocaust.

The Israel–Arab conflict simmered, flaring up frequently such as in 1956 during the Suez Campaign and 1967 when

⊙ INDEPENDENCE

Despite the Holocaust, the UN first rejected the idea of an independent Jewish state in Palestine, but after diplomatic lobbying by Ben Gurion, the partition plan dividing Palestine into Jewish and Arab states was passed in 1947. Israel declared independence the following year. The armies of the entire Arab world attacked Israel but when an armistice was declared, Israel had made territorial gains in the Galilee and Negev and incorporated West Jerusalem as its capital. The Arab world enlarged Israel's population by expelling their Jewish communities, so that the Israel's Jewish population, boosted to 717,000 by Holocaust survivors by 1948, had doubled to 1.5 million by 1955. Israel retained an Arab minority (today 23% of the population) while hundreds of thousands of others escaped the conflict by fleeing to neighbouring Arab countries, creating the Palestinian refugee problem, which remains unresolved today.

Israel struck first after Egypt's President Nasser blockaded Israel's Red Sea port of Eilat and spoke of "driving the Jews into the sea". Israel captured the Sinai and Gaza from Egypt, the Golan Heights from Syria, and most significantly, the West Bank, including East Jerusalem, from Jordan. The Sinai was returned to Egypt after another round of fighting in 1973 and a peace treaty that was concluded in 1979 and the West Bank became the focus of the conflict.

While Ben Gurion's socialist party and his successors up to Yitzhak Rabin and Shimon Peres remained in power until 1977, Israel was ready to relinquish the West Bank. But then Menachem Begin's right-wing nationalist Likud party won power and began to settle the West Bank, the historic heart-land of biblical Israel with cities like Hebron.

The Palestinian movement had come into its own from 1967 onwards. Yassir Arafat, formerly imprisoned by Syria, was released to head the Palestinian Liberation Organisation (PLO). After a campaign of terror and the first intifada, a local upris-ing in the West Bank and Gaza, Israel and the PLO signed a peace agreement in 1993, which was opposed by extremists on

⊙ PARLIAMENTARY DEMOCRACY

A socialist who was greatly influenced by the Soviet Union, Ben Gurion, the undisputed leader and architect of the fledg-ling state, opted for a UK-style parliamentary democracy upon gaining independence. The 120-seat Knesset remains sovereign today, with elections at least every four years. Nevertheless, the civil service and a highly centralized so-cialist economy had a Soviet flavor to it.

Israeli Navy boat on patrol in the Red Sea during the Six-Day War, 1967

both sides. Israel's Prime Minister Yitzhak Rabin was assassinated by a right-wing Jewish gunman in 1995 and Palestinian terror attacks on Israel continued.

In 2000, Arafat and Israeli Prime Minister Ehud Barak failed to hammer out a final peace agreement. Barak agreed to relinquish almost all the West Bank and Gaza and cede land in the Negev to the Palestinians. But Arafat demanded the right of return for all Palestinian refugees to Israel – a move that would have meant the end of the Jewish majority in Israel.

Hostilities resumed in the second intifada and to counter incessant attacks from suicide bombers, Israel's government, led by Ariel Sharon, built a separation wall between Israel and the West Bank. Israel unilaterally withdrew from Gaza in 2005 but continued rocket attacks on Israel from the Hamas-led Gaza government led to major Israeli military operations against the Palestinians in 2009 and 2014.

Start-up Nation

Israel's population of 9 million has a highly developed economy. Tech is by far Israel's biggest industry and the country is famous for its hundreds of start-ups in such areas as IT, AI, defence electronics, medical devices, biotech, and much more.

In 2018, tensions were reignited after a covert Israeli operation into Gaza went wrong, resulting in fatalities on both sides. Eventually, a ceasefire was agreed in November.

With similar low-level hostilities between Israel and the Palestinians continuing, coupled with the stance of Israel's right-wing Orthodox and nationalist-led coalition, headed by Benjamin Netanyahu, peace seems more elusive than ever today.

Start-up business in Jerusalem

HISTORICAL LANDMARKS

10,000 BC Some of the world's first farming settlements are established

2000 BC Abraham moves from Mesopotamia to Be'er Sheva

1280 BC Moses leads the Israelites out of Egypt towards Canaan

1000 BC King David builds Jerusalem as his capital and his son Solomon builds the First Temple

520 BC Jews return to Jerusalem from the Babylonian exile and build the Second Temple

63 BC The Romans conquer Judea and in the following decades destroy the Second Temple and exile the Jews.

30 A preacher from Galilee called Jesus Christ is crucified in Jerusalem.

325 Roman Emperor Constantine converts to Christianity and sends his mother to the Holy Land to identify the sacred sites.

637 The Muslims capture Jerusalem and build the Dome of the Rock.

1099 The Crusaders capture the Holy Land.

1291 The Mamelukes defeat the Crusaders at Akko, taking control of Palestine.

1516 The Ottoman Turks capture Palestine and Suleiman the Magnificent builds the walls around Jerusalem.

1917 The British become the rulers of Palestine and issue the Balfour Declaration that it should become a Jewish State.

1948 Israel declares Independence.

1967 Israel captures the West Bank, Gaza, Sinai and Golan Heights during the Six-Day War.

1977 29 years of Labor party rule end as the nationalist Likud wins power.

1995 Israeli Prime Minister Yitzhak Rabin is assassinated.

2000 Peace talks with the Palestinians break down and the Second Intifada begins.

2005 Israel withdraws from Gaza.

2017 President Donald Trump announces that the US officially recognises Jerusalem as the capital of Israel, reigniting tensions in the region.

2018 Israeli forces and Hamas clash in Gaza after a covert operation goes wrong, and an Israeli officer is killed.

At the edge of Makhtesh Ramon
Crater, in the Negev Desert

WHERE TO GO

Arriving at Ben Gurion Airport, you can go eastwards up into the hills to Jerusalem, with its history and religion and down through the desert landscapes to the Dead Sea, the lowest point on earth. Further south through the Arava desert is the Red Sea resort of Eilat with its tropical waters and colorful marine life and coral formations. Or you can travel westwards to Tel Aviv, Israel's bustling, economic capital, a brash place of gleaming high-tech office towers, golden beaches and a pulsating nightlife. The coast extends northwards to the former Roman capital of Caesarea, the port city of Haifa with the resplendent Bahá'í Gardens stretching up Mount Carmel and the former Crusader stronghold of Akko. Also in the north are the rolling hills of the Galilee, the region where Jesus Christ spent most of his life. This is a magical, mystical region where the River Jordan feeds into the Sea of Galilee beneath the Golan Heights and majestic, snow-capped Mount Hermon.

From east to west, Israel (including the Palestinian territories) is less than 100km (60 miles) wide. From north to south, it is 500km (310 miles) – a small but geographically diverse country and it is possible in the winter to ski on Mount Hermon in the morning and go scuba diving in the Red Sea in the afternoon.

JERUSALEM

The Holy City of **Jerusalem** ❶ is sacred to Jews, Christians and Muslims. It is also home to Israeli national institutions such as the Knesset (Parliament) and Israel Museum. It is also a city of strife, with the Palestinians in the east of the city demanding it as their capital. However, despite all this religion and politics, the city – 800 meters (2,625ft) above sea level – surrounded by forests to the west and deserts to the east is a delight to visit, with stirring mountain panoramas and a bustling nightlife. Many of the sights are within walking distance of each other and there are good bus and tram and services.

THE OLD CITY

The Old City houses sacred shrines, a bustling market and is divided into the Jewish, Christian, Armenian and Muslim quarters. The main entrance is the **Jaffa Gate Ⓐ**, located by the **Tower of David Museum of the History of Jerusalem Ⓑ** (Sun–Thu 10am–4pm, in summer until 5pm and 10pm on Sun, Tue and Thu, Sat 10am–2pm; www.towerofdavid.org.il), which

Old City, Jerusalem

has displays describing the tumultuous history of the city. A sound and light show with a separate entrance projects the city's history onto the Old City walls at night (tel: 02-626 5333 or book online www. towerofdavid.org.il).

The Municipal Tourist Information Office is just inside the Jaffa Gate (Sun– Thu 8.30am–5pm) and nearby is the **Christian Information Office** (Mon– Fri 8.30am–5.30pm, Sat 8.30am–12.30pm). Slightly further along from the

Jaffa Gate is the entrance to the **Souk (Bazaar) ⓒ** where friendly shopkeepers will assault you with trinkets at 'special prices'. At the end of the alleyway El Bazar, turn right onto Ha-Kardo for the Jewish Quarter.

The Jewish Quarter was rebuilt after 1967. **Ha-Kardo ⓓ** is a submerged pedestrian byway that ran along the main north–south axis and was built by the Romans in AD 70. Nearby is the great **Hurva Synagogue ⓔ**, which was recently rebuilt in 19th-century neo-Byzantine style. At the end of Tif'eret Yisra'el is a fascinating archeological site: the **Burnt House ⓕ** (Sun–Thu 9am–5pm, Fri 9am–1pm), which was the residence of the priestly Bar-Kathros clan during the Jewish revolt against Rome.

> ### Sexual Segregation
>
> The area in front of the wall is divided into separate sections for male and female prayer. Non-Orthodox Jewish women often challenge the status-quo by bringing Torah scrolls into the female side, antagonizing the local rabbinate.

The Western Wall

The steps at the end of Tif'eret Yisra'el lead down to the most important site in Judaism: the **Western Wall ⓖ** (always open; free), which is made from massive carved-stone blocks that date back to the Herodian era. A retaining wall for the western side of the Temple Mount, it is the only remnant of the Temple complex to survive demolition by the Romans and has inspired Jews for 2,000 years.

The Temple Mount

The **Temple Mount** (Sun–Thu 7.30–11.30am and 12.30–1.30pm; closed during Ramadan, and to non-Muslims on Fri and

Muslim holidays; free), which Muslims call **Haram esh-Sharif** (the Venerable Sanctuary) is the biblical Mount Moriah where Abraham nearly sacrificed Isaac, where the First and Second Temples once stood, and where the golden Dome of the Rock and the silvery El-Aqsa Mosque now stand.

The most eye-catching structure on Haram esh-Sharif is the **Dome of the Rock ⓗ**. The outside of the edifice, which is a shrine and not a mosque, is a fantasia of marble, mosaics and stained glass, painted tiles and quotations from the Quran, all capped by the gold-plated aluminium dome.

The inside of the Dome of the Rock focuses on the huge boulder called the **Kubbet es-Sakhra**, the sacred rock on which Abraham was said to have prepared the sacrifice of Isaac. It is also the spot on which, during his mystical journey to Jerusalem, Mohammed is said to have mounted his steed and ascended to heaven. Since 2000, non-Muslims have not been permitted to visit the interiors of the Dome of the Rock or the El-Aqsa Mosque. The silver-capped mosque to the south

⦿ THE CORE OF THE CONFLICT

The Temple Mount is Jerusalem's most disputed land. The Arab nations are determined that an Islamic flag must fly over the site and Israel leaves administration of Haram esh-Sharif entirely to Muslim officials called the Wakf. Israeli Border Police provide security in cooperation with Arab policemen. Israel's Chief Rabbinate has banned Jews from visiting the Temple Mount, because somewhere on the hill is the site of the ancient Temple's Holy of Holies, the inner sanctuary which only the High Priest was allowed to enter. However many nationalist Israelis provocatively hold prayer services on the Mount.

is **El-Aqsa** . Able to accommodate up to 5,000 worshippers, El-Aqsa has a functional design and straddles vast underground chambers known as **Solomon's Stables**.

By the Western Wall is the entrance to the **Western Wall Tunnel** ❶ (Sun–Thu 7.20am until 10pm, Fri 7.20am–12pm tel: 02-627133; advance booking required). Archeologists have dug out a 2,000-year-old street leading along the rim of the Temple Mount several hundred meters northwards to the Via Dolorosa.

Dome of the Rock

Via Dolorosa

The **Via Dolorosa**, one of the most sacred routes in Christianity, marks Christ's journey to his crucifixion, his burial and his resurrection. Begin at the **Convent of St Anne** just inside from **St Stephen's Gate** (Lions Gate; open Mon–Sat), the best-preserved Crusader church in the Holy Land, with a crypt designated as Mary's birthplace.

The **First Station of the Cross**, where Jesus was sentenced, is to the left inside the courtyard of the Umariyah School. The **Second Station**, where Jesus received the Cross, is opposite, on the street outside the **Chapel of Condemnation** and the **Church of the Flagellation** ❸. It was here that Jesus was scourged and had the crown of thorns placed on his head. In the nearby **Convent of the Sisters of Zion** is a huge underground chamber called the Lithostrotos (Mon–Sat 8.30am–12.30pm, 2–4.30pm), said to be where Pilate judged Jesus. Outside is the **Ecce Homo Arch**, which some maintain was constructed by Emperor Hadrian in the 2nd century.

The **Third Station**, where Jesus fell with the Cross, is commemorated by a column in a wall on Ha-Gai (El Wad), which the Via Dolorosa traverses. Just beyond is the **Fourth Station**, where Jesus encountered Mary. On this site is the **Armenian Catholic Church of Our Lady of the Spasm**, which has a notable Byzantine mosaic in its crypt. The Via Dolorosa at this point becomes a steep lane ascending to the right from Ha-Gai. The nearby **Fifth Station** is where Simon the Cyrenian helped Jesus carry the Cross. The **Sixth Station**, at the **House of St Veronica**, where Veronica cleansed the face of Jesus. Where the Via Dolorosa bisects the souk's Khan ez-Zeit bazaar is the **Seventh Station**, where Jesus fell again.

The Church of the Holy Sepulchre – built on the location of the Crucifixion and Christ's tomb – and the last Stations of the Cross are close by. The **Eighth Station** is outside the **Greek Orthodox Chapel of St Charalampos**, and at the **Coptic Patriarchate** ❶ compound off the Khan ez-Zeit bazaar, a pillar marks the **Ninth Station**, where Jesus stumbled for the third time.

The Church of the Holy Sepulchre

The **Church of the Holy Sepulchre** Ⓜ (daily, dawn to dusk) was rebuilt by the Crusaders in the 12th century and added to over the centuries. Several Christian communities share the church, and are responsible for scrupulously specified areas. Church fathers have battled in the past over who cleans which steps. With its gloomy interior, competing chants and multiple

Inside the Church of the Holy Sepulchre

aromas of incense, the church exudes magnificence. The focal points are the hillock where the Crucifixion took place (called Golgotha, from Hebrew; or Calvary, from Latin) and the tomb where Jesus was laid to rest.

Stairs to the right inside the door to the church lead up to **Calvary**. The **Tenth Station**, where Jesus was stripped of his garments, is marked by a floor mosaic. The next three stations are located at Latin and Greek altars on this same level, within a few paces of each other. They mark the nailing of Jesus to the Cross, the placing of the Cross, and the removal of Christ's body. The **Fourteenth Station** is below the Holy Sepulchre: the tomb is downstairs under the church's main rotunda.

Outside the Holy Sepulchre there are many churches. The tower of the **Lutheran Church of the Redeemer** is the highest point in the Old City (Mon–Sat 9am–5pm), offering a magnificent view. From the Church of the Holy Sepulchre the main thoroughfare northwards leads to the **Damascus Gate**. From here – as from most of the city gates – there is access to the **Ramparts Walk** (daily 9am), a walk around the top of the city walls that provides marvellous views.

The Armenian Quarter

Entrance to the **Armenian Quarter** ⊙, a walled enclave within a walled city is permitted only on Mon–Fri 6.30–7.30am and 3–3.40pm, Sat–Sun 6.30–9.30am. It can be reached by turning right inside the **Jaffa Gate**. A modest doorway leads to the 12th-century **St James's Cathedral**, one of the most impressive churches in the Old City. Nearby is the **Armenian Museum**, a graceful cloister housing a collection of manuscripts and artifacts.

Ramparts Walk

OUTSIDE THE OLD CITY

The streets outside the Damascus Gate form Arab Jerusalem's city center. The **East Jerusalem Bus Station**, just opposite, operates buses to points in the West Bank. Several hundred meters from Damascus Gate, along Derekh Shkem, is the **Garden Tomb P** (Mon–Sat 9am–noon, 2–5.30pm; free). Within a sumptuous garden, this is a dual-chambered cave that Anglicans and Protestants claim could have been the tomb of Jesus. The Garden Tomb is situated on a hill which, if viewed from the east, suggests the shape of a skull, thus the belief that it was actually here where Christ was crucified and buried.

The hill to the west of the Damascus Gate is dominated by the splendid 19th-century **Notre Dame de France Hospice Q**, which is opposite the **New Gate**. The grandiose, ornate French architecture suggests that pilgrims that made the journey did not suffer deprivation and the building now houses a luxury hotel and a cordon bleu French restaurant.

Follow the Old City walls and you'll see the Mamila mall on the right. This 19th-century district of workshops has been transformed into a complex of luxury apartments with some of the original buildings, such as the St Vincent orphanage, intact. The main street is a pedestrian shopping mall with outdoor cafés overlooking the Old City and fashionable stores. To the south is **Sultan's Pool R**, formerly a reservoir that has been converted into an atmospheric amphitheater for outdoor concerts beneath the Old City walls.

Mount Zion

Mount Zion S can be reached along the gardens south of the **Jaffa Gate**, or from **Zion Gate.** Within the Diaspora Yeshiva complex is the site of **King David's Tomb T** (Sun–Thu 8am–5pm, Fri 8am–1pm; free), although some archeologists doubt its

A heavy price

Legend has it that Suleiman the Magnificent, the Ottoman ruler who completed construction of the Old City walls in 1541, executed his chief architect for forgetting to include Mount Zion inside the walls.

authenticity. Above the tomb is the Coenaculum (daily 8am–5pm; tel: 02-6713597 free), believed to be the Room of the Last Supper.

The City of David (Sun–Thu 8am–5pm, until 7pm in summer, Fri 8pm–1pm, until 3pm in summer; www.cityofdavid.org.il) excavations are on the steep hillside outside the Dung Gate. Around 1000 BC, King David captured the city and made it his capital. At the foot of the slope is the **Gihon Spring** , which was Jerusalem's only water supply at the time. Since the spring was located in a cave on the floor of the valley, Jerusalemites were in danger of being cut off from their water when the city was attacked. But the stunning engineering project known as Hezekiah's Tunnel carried out by King Hezekiah about 300 years later, connected the Gihon Spring to the Silwan Pool inside the city some 580 yards down the valley.

The Mount of Olives

It is believed that Jesus made his triumphal entry into Jerusalem from the Mount of Olives. This hill, with its breathtaking view of the Old City, is a predominately Jewish cemetery dating back to biblical times and is still in use today. Jews and Christians believe that the Messiah will lead the resurrected from here into Jerusalem via the Old City's bricked up Golden Gate, which faces the mount.

At the foot of the mount is the handsome **Church of All Nations**, (open daily; free), noted for its Byzantine-style mosaic facade. Adjoining is the **Garden of Gethsemane**  where Jesus was betrayed and adjacent is **Mary's Tomb** (open daily 6am–5pm; free). Midway down the stairs of the 5th-century chapel are niches said to hold the remains of Mary's parents, Joachim and Anne, and her husband Joseph. Among the most notable churches on the way up the mount is the **Russian Orthodox Church of Mary Magdalene** (Tue and Thu am only; free) built in 1886 with its golden onion-domes. At the top of the Mount of Olives is the Seven Arches Hotel and the classic picture-postcard view of Jerusalem's Old City.

NEW JERUSALEM

Along the ridge is **Mount Scopus**, the site of the **Hebrew University**, which was inaugurated in 1925, although most of the buildings you see today were built after 1967. Among the most impressive sites here is the amphitheater, which offers an awesome view of the rolling Judean Hills. Between Mount Scopus and the New City is the **American Colony Hotel,** Jerusalem's oldest hotel and a favourite haunt of foreign journalists because of its neutral location between East and West Jerusalem.

Nearby is **Me'a She'arim**, the most

Me'a She'arim neighborhood

famous ultra-Orthodox Jewish neighborhood in the country. Built in 1875, the neighborhood has retained much of the flavor of a *shtetl* (a traditional Jewish village or town that existed in Europe before the Holocaust). The Jews who live here speak Yiddish and wear the traditional styles: side-curls, heavy, black garments for the men and shawls for the women. Signs warning that "immodest" female dress is not tolerated should be taken seriously, with offenders often being spat at and cursed. **Ha-Nevi'im** (The Street of the Prophets), which runs parallel to the south of Me'a She'arim, is famed for its Ottoman architecture and beautiful buildings.

Jaffa Road

Ha-Nevi'im's western end meets Jaffa (Yafo) Road at its midpoint between the city entrance and Jaffa Gate. Jaffa Road was the historic main axis for traffic, from the gate towards Jaffa, which today has been pedestrianized except for trams. Leaving the Old City behind, Jaffa Road passes the new City Hall municipal complex and plaza and the adjacent **Russian Compound** purchased by Tsar Alexander II for the Russian pilgrims who flocked to Jerusalem. This complex, including the handsome green-domed **Cathedral of the Holy Trinity** and the **Russian Consulate**, was completed in 1864 and marked the first notable Russian presence outside the Old City. The compound has been largely bought by the Israeli government, and the buildings house law courts, a police station, and a plethora of bars.

DOWNTOWN

Across Jaffa Road are the winding lanes of **Nakhalat Shiva**, Jerusalem's second-oldest residential suburb, which was founded in the 1860s and has been delightfully renovated since. At the hub is **Kikar Tsiyon (Zion Square)**, a popular venue for both young Israelis to meet and political demonstrations. Ben Yehuda, the pedestrian avenue that begins at Zion Square was once the heart of the city's café life. The street is still popular but the new Mamilla Mall, the Germany Colony, Russian Compound and especially Makhane Yehuda market offer a more vibrant night life.

Ha-Melekh George (King George V Street), which cuts across Ben Yehuda at the top of the street, is the city center's main north-south axis. To the south is the **Jerusalem Great Synagogue** and next door is the former seat of the chief Rabbinate of Israel, Heikhal Shlomo. From Ha-Melekh George turn left down Gershon Agron, which borders **Independence Park**, a refreshing green expanse in the city center. David

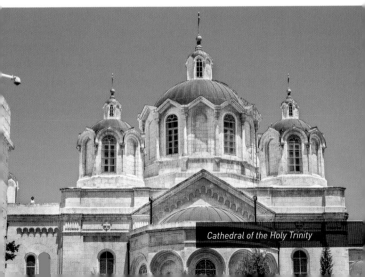

Cathedral of the Holy Trinity

The Montefiore Windmill

ha-Melekh (King David Street) hosts two of Jerusalem's most-celebrated edifices. The YMCA, completed in 1933, was the work of Shreve, Lamb & Harmon, who were simultaneously designing the Empire State Building. Its 36-meter (118-ft) tower offers an outstanding view of Jerusalem. The **King David Hotel** opposite was built with old-world grandeur by Egyptian Jews in 1930. It is customary for visiting heads of state to stay at the King David or the nearby David's Citadel Hotel.

SOUTH OF THE CENTER

Just south is the **Montefiore Windmill,** a conspicuous landmark built by the British philanthropist Sir Moses Montefiore that now houses a modest museum (Sun–Thu 9am–4pm, Fri 9am–1pm; free). The windmill is at the heart of the first Jewish suburb built outside the Old City. Called Mishkenot Sh'Ananim (Dwellings of Tranquillity), the long, block-like structure was built in 1860 by Montefiore and he later expanded the quarter, calling it Yemin Moshe. In the 1970s, Yemin Moshe was revitalised as an artists' colony, and today its twee stone houses command some of the highest prices in the city. Montefiore built the windmill to provide flour for the residents. Nearby is the Scottish **St Andrew's Church,** built in 1329 to house King Bruce's heart, which never made it to the Holy Land.

Opposite is the former railway station opened in 1892. Trains no longer run and the area has been converted into a popular complex of cafés and restaurants. The disused railway line between here and Malkah to the south has been transformed into an attractive park for pedestrians and cyclists. Continue onto the tree-lined streets of the **German Colony,** founded in 1873 by German Templars. The central street is Emek Refa'im, a fashionable thoroughfare of stores, restaurants and cafés leading to the Talpiyot industrial zone, a less salubrious mix of discount shops, wedding halls and night clubs. To the east is the **Armon Hanatziv Promenade,** which offers a splendid view of the Old City, also known as the Hill of the Evil Counsel, as it is where Judas Iscariot is said to have received his 30 pieces of silver for betraying Jesus Christ.

Western Entrance

The Western Entrance to Jerusalem is distinguished by **the Bridge of Chords** – a harp-like structure designed by international architect Santiago Calitrava. Nearby are the Central Bus Station and new railway station. To the east, is the **Supreme Court** (tours in English Sun–Thu at noon; tel: 02-6759612) – an impressive edifice that uses light, shade and glass to great effect. Just south, past the Bank of Israel and the Prime Minister's Office, is the **Knesset** (Israel's parliament) (open Mon–Wed during debates, Sun and Thu 8.30am–2.30pm; for guided tours tel: 02-6753420; www.knesset.gov.il). The 120-seat chamber is the symbol of Israel's democratic system and the interior includes a tapestry designed by Marc Chagall.

The Israel Museum, (Sat–Mon, Wed & Thu 10am–5pm, Tues 4–9pm, Fri 10am–2pm; www.imj.org.il) is a block from

Shrine of the Book

the Knesset, and is Israel's national museum and an international showcase for art, archeology and Judaica. Its most famous exhibit is the Shrine of the Book which displays the Dead Sea Scrolls – scraps of tattered parchment from the oldest known copy of the Old Testament. There is also a Model of the Second Temple, which conveys how vast the Second Temple complex must have been.

Opposite are two more museums: **The Bible Lands Museum** (Sun–Thu 9.30am–5.30pm, Wed 9.30am–9.30pm, Fri 9.30am–2pm; www.blmj.org), displaying artifacts dating from biblical times, and the hands-on **Bloomfield Science Museum** (Mon–Thu 10am–6pm, Fri 10am–2pm, Sat 10am–4pm; www.mada.org.il), an imaginative experience popular with children.

To the west of the Valley of the Cross is the Botanical Gardens, which is set by a pretty lake. It is part of the **Hebrew University's Givat Ram Campus,** which includes the university's science faculties and the Jewish National and University Library (Sun–Thu 9am–7pm, Fri 9am–1pm; free), one of the world's largest libraries and where Albert Einstein worked on his theory of relativity.

Away from the government center, Israel's political pulse can be better felt in the nearby **Makhane Yehuda Market.** The vendors who offer a tempting array of fresh fruit, vegetables, nuts, and spices will also hawk their readily available opinions. At night, the market morphs into the heart of the city's night-life, buzzing with restaurants, cafés, and bars.

Yad Vashem

The Yad Vashem Holocaust History Museum (Sun–Thu 9am–5pm, Fri 9am–2pm; www.yadvashem.org.il; free) is a striking memorial to the 6 million Jews murdered by the Nazis. The complex also includes the Hall of Remembrance engraved with the names of 21 death camps.

⊘ BETHLEHEM

The city of Christ's birth is just 9 km (6 miles) south of **Jerusalem**, although involves crossing into the Palestinian Authority (bring your passport) and changing buses or taxis at the border. In Manger Square is the **Church of the Nativity** (open daily dawn–dusk). The original basilica was built in 325 by Emperor Constantine the Great and the foundation for it is the crypt revered in Christian tradition as the place where Jesus was born.

Beyond the vestibule is the nave; much of this interior dates from Emperor Justinian's rebuilding in the 6th century. Downstairs, is the **Grotto of the Nativity**, where inscribed in Latin is 'Here Jesus Christ was born of the Virgin Mary'. Next door is the **Chapel of the Manger**, where Mary placed the new-born child. Adjoining is the Catholic **St Catherine's**, from which Bethlehem's Midnight Mass on Christmas Eve is broadcast worldwide.

19km (13 miles) further south is Hebron, where Abraham is buried in the Cave of the Patriarchs, a constant flashpoint in the Israel-Palestinian conflict.

Chagall's colorful stained-glass windows

Ein Kerem, the picturesque neighborhood nestling beneath Yad Vashem is rich in religious history. Sites include the Franciscan Church of the Visitation, on the spot where the Virgin Mary visited Elizabeth, John the Baptist's mother, and the central Spring of the Vineyard (also known as Mary's Fountain), which gave the village its name. The Church of St John, mosaics, and a grotto mark the traditional birthplace of the Baptist. Hadassah Hospital, above the village, is known for Marc Chagall's stained-glass windows, depicting the 12 tribes of Israel.

TEL AVIV

Tel Aviv ②, Israel's commercial capital, oozes energy. It is the city that never stops, from its golden beaches and glistening high-tech office towers, to its innovative culinary and cultural scene and pulsating nightlife. Tel Aviv itself has a population of 550,000, and is at the heart of a metropolitan area called Gush Dan, which is home to over 4 million people.

In 1909, the sand dunes north of Jaffa were transformed into an affluent garden suburb, although Tel Aviv is far more than a century old. Biblical Jaffa is one of the world's oldest ports and Neve Tsedek, which links Jaffa to Tel Aviv and was established in 1887. Tel Aviv was further developed in the 1930s by German immigrants fleeing Nazi persecution who introduced Bauhaus architecture. David Ben-Gurion declared the city's independence here in 1948 but in the ensuing years, the city became shabby as waves of penniless immigrants arrived. But Israel's famous high-tech industry and start-up culture have seen the city emerge as one of the world's financial centers.

NORTH TEL AVIV

Entering Tel Aviv from the north, you'll see some of the city's wealthiest suburbs surrounding Tel Aviv University campus, which contains the **Museum of the Jewish People** (Bet Hatfutsot) **A** (open Sun–Tue & Thu 10am–4pm, Wed 10am–6pm Fri 9am–1pm; www.bh.org.il). Founded in 1979, it was a departure from conventional museums, telling the story of the Jewish Diaspora rather than exhibiting artifacts. The core museum was recently reopened with a new cutting edge design. Nearby in Ramat Aviv is the sprawling **Eretz Israel Museum B** (open Sun–Wed 10am–4pm, Thu 10am–8pm, Fri & Sat 10am–2pm; www.eretzmuseum.org.il), which is the region's most comprehensive storehouse of archeological, anthropological, and historical findings. The **River Yarkon C** is lined with rambling parkland and marks the northern border of the city proper. To the south is Little Old Tel Aviv where three of the city's major north-south roads begin: Ha-Yarkon, Ben Yehuda and Dizengoff, and Tel Aviv Port, closed in 1965 and reopened a

Tel Aviv Seafront Promenade

Stretching 15km (9 miles) from Tel Baruch in the north to Jaffa in the south, the seafront pedestrian path also has a cycle track and passes all the city's major beaches.

decade ago as a popular center with fashionable stores, restaurants, bars, and clubs.

To the south stretches Independence Gardens, a strip of green offering a stirring view of the Mediterranean from its cliffs. Just inland, in Ben Gurion Boulevard, home to **Ben Gurion House** (Sun, Mon 8am–5pm, Tues–Thu 8am–3pm, Sat 8am–1pm). This was the home of Israel's first prime minister and today a public museum housing the personal mementos of David Ben Gurion.

CENTRAL TEL AVIV

The Hilton also marks the start of the city's central hotel district. The marina rents out boats and equipment for water sports and is overlooked by **Kikar Atarim** , which is slated for redevelopment. The coastline here is dominated by an imposing row of hotels overlooking the city's most popular beaches. Marking the end of the hotel line to the south are the Dan Panorama and David Intercontinental, just a short distance from Jaffa.

Inland from these two hotels is the **Yemenite Quarter** , with Arab-style stone houses and excellent restaurants. **The Carmel Market** adjacent to the south is always crowded with shoppers and is a medley of colors, smells and sounds. A large variety of exotic fruits, vegetables, herbs and spices, as well as clothes and shoes, can be found here at bargain prices.

By the eastern entrance to the Carmel Market on Allenby Street is a pedestrian mall called Nakhalat Binyamin where on Tuesdays and Fridays, arts and crafts traders bring their wares to sell – a great place for present or souvenir shopping.

To the south is **Neve Tsedek** , which was founded in 1887 and is a picturesque maze of narrow streets flanked by low-built houses. The quarter has undergone gentrification and property here now commands astronomical prices, with Roman Abramovich paying $30 million for a home here in 2015. At the heart of the neighborhood is the **Suzan Dalal Center**. Originally the city's first girls' school, it is today the home of the Batsheva Dance Company and the Inbal Dance Company amid a magnificent plaza dotted with orange trees. Also in Neve Tsedek, the former Jaffa railway station has been converted into an attractive cultural and exhibition center.

JAFFA (YAFO)

Jaffa is one of the world's oldest cities and retained its biblical flavor. The cedars of Lebanon used by King Solomon to build the Temple in Jerusalem were shipped to Jaffa, Jonah set sail on his ill-fated voyage from here and the raising of Tabitha from the dead was per-formed by Peter when he stayed at the Jaffa home of Simon the Tanner.

Old Jaffa was recon-structed in 1963, with cob-bled paths and winding alleys twisting through the massive stone fortifi-cations surrounding the city with an artists' colony and galleries, craft shops, restaurants, and night-clubs. The **Old Port ❶** still houses local fishermen, as well as several charm-ing quayside restaurants. Old Jaffa begins at the

Old Jaffa port

Ottoman Clock Tower **J** on Yefet facing the former Turkish prison, now a luxury boutique hotel called the Setai. Right on Mifrats Shlomo is the **Jaffa Museum of Antiquities** **K** (Sun–Thu 9am–1pm, Tues also 4–7pm, Sat 10am–2pm), where archeological exhibits from many years of excavations trace the city's development. On the other side of Yefet is Jaffa's famous Flea Market, which specialises in antiques, copperware, jewelry, and second-hand junk.

The Franciscan **St Peter's Church** **M** is further along, at Kedumim Square. The St Louis Monastery in the courtyard was named after the French king who arrived here at the head of a Crusade in 1147. Napoleon also relaxed here after conquering Jaffa. The top of the hill, past the Pisgah Park, **Horoscope Path** is the best view of Tel Aviv from Jaffa. Down an alleyway to the right of Kedumim Square is Simon the Tanner's House (daily 8am–7pm) where, in addition to performing miracles, Peter is believed to have received divine instruction to preach to non-Jews. To the northeast of Jaffa lies **Florentine** **N**, a bustling Bohemian neighborhood undergoing gentrification, which includes the Levinsky spice market.

Rothschild Boulevard

Immediately north of Jaffa are the original streets of Tel Aviv's garden suburb, which today house the financial district. Beneath the Shalom Tower on Herzl, for many years the tallest building in Israel, is the western end of **Rothschild Boulevard** **O**. Built in 1910 over a dried riverbed, the boulevard was once Tel Aviv's most elegant address. After decades of decline, it is once again elegant and expensive, its central promenade dotted with trees, benches, and refreshment kiosks as well as a cycle path, and its buildings embrace an eclectic jumble of styles.

The public museum, **Independence Hall** , is at number 16, and is housed in the former residence of the city's first mayor, Meir Dizengoff. The Declaration of Independence was signed here on 15 May 1948, and it was also the first home of the Knesset (parliament). Breuer House at number 46 was built in 1922; it has tiny decorative balconies, a pagoda-like wooden roof, a minaret,

Rothschild Boulevard

and a large enclosed garden. On the verge of demolition in 1948, it was saved when the Soviet ambassador requested it for his headquarters. It served as the Soviet Embassy until 1953, when diplomatic relations with the USSR were severed. Renovated in the 1990s, it now houses Sotheby's Israel offices. Typical Bauhaus-style buildings can be seen at numbers 89, 91 and 140, and on nearby Engel, recently converted into a pedestrian mall.

Sheinkin ⓠ, which stretches eastwards off Rothschild Boulevard, is home to many fashion stores. At its western end is the **Betsal'el Market**, a place to find discount quality fashion items and bric-a-brac. At the northern end of Rothschild is Tel Aviv's premier cultural complex including the **Ha-Bimah Theater**, the **Mann Auditorium** (home to the Israel Philharmonic Orchestra) and the **Rubinstein Pavilion** ⓡ (Mon, Wed 10am–4pm, Tue, Thu 10am–10pm; Fri 10am–2pm Sat.

Restaurants in Dizengoff

10am–4pm; tel: 03-528 7196). A branch of the **Tel Aviv Museum of Art** ⑤ (same hours as pavilion; www.tamuseum.co.il), which is Israel's biggest art museum, can be found nearby at Sha'ul Ha-Melekh.

DIZENGOFF

This arts complex is at the start of **Dizengoff** ⑦, once the city's most fashionable thoroughfare and although less grand today, still one of Tel Aviv's principal streets. Dizengoff Square was recently renovated to recreate the traffic roundabout that was at the heart of Dizengoff in its heyday between the 1930s and 60s. At its eastern end, Dizengoff leads into Kaplan Street. On the south side of Kaplan are the red-slated roofs of the German Templar Colony (1870–1939), known as Sarona, and recently developed into a complex of stores, restaurants, and a food market. On the north side is the Israel Defence Forces HQ, marked by a huge concrete antenna tower.

At the end of Kaplan is the heart of Israel's high-tech industry, which is marked by a series of tall office towers. These include the **Azrieli Center** with three towers – one round, one triangular, and one square. The Azrieli Center, with direct access to the Shalom railway station, is one of Israel's largest shopping malls. To the south is the Azrieli Sarona tower, currently Israel's tallest building but soon to be surpassed by several high-rises under construction to the north.

Back westwards to Ibn Gabirol, the road leads northwards to the city's central square next to municipality building. It was here, on what is now called **Yitzhak Rabin Square ⓤ**, that Prime Minister Yitzhak Rabin was assassinated in 1995 after a huge demonstration in support of the peace process. East along Jabotinski Street is Kikar Hamedina, a huge roundabout with home to manty of Israel's most expensive fashion stores.

Further east, a dense forest of high-rise buildings marks the **Diamond Exchange district**, in adjoining Ramat Gan rather than Tel Aviv. The gleaming office blocks contain not only one of the world's biggest diamond trading center, but also high-tech enterprises. **The Diamond Exchange ⓥ** has a museum (Sun–Thu 10am–4pm, Fri 8am–noon; tel; www.diamond-il. co.il), which tells the story of diamonds.

The original architects would not have approved. Developed in the 1920s, Bauhaus architecture was simple and socialistic as new technologies provided cheaper homes on less land.

⊘ WHITE CITY

Tel Aviv is a Unesco World Heritage Site because of its unique collection of Bauhaus buildings. The city has more than 1,500 such buildings, by far the largest number of any location worldwide, with most of them to be found in Rothschild Boulevard, and the roads to the north. The understated cubic style is often hidden behind trees and urban grime. But many of the buildings have been restored to their former glory, and property developers are rehabilitating many more, usually adding on expensive penthouses.

Hitler halted the Bauhaus school of architecture because it he viewed it as 'un-German'. Many of the architects who left Germany were Jews who came to Tel Aviv and influenced the city's architecture. Pictures from the 1930s show Bauhaus in its full glory and reveal why Tel Aviv is called the White City. Engel Street, a mews off Rothschild Boulevard, and Dizengoff Square are both excellent places to appreciate the full effect of Tel Aviv's Bauhaus architecture.

THE GALILEE AND GOLAN

In this relatively compact region of rolling green hills and mountain streams, Christians can retrace the steps of Jesus, while Jews can reflect on the region that produced their greatest mystics. On the main artery that linked the ancient empires, the Galilee has been a battleground for Egyptian pharaohs, biblical kings, Romans and Jews, Christians and Muslims, Britain and Turkey.

Ruins at Tel Megiddo

Jewish pioneers established the country's first kibbutzim here, which mushroomed to cover much of this region, where Arab and Druze villages lie nestled in the hills. A circular tour of the entire Galilee and Golan covers less than 402km (250 miles) but is crammed incredible history, sacred sites, diverse inhabitants, and breathtaking landscapes.

JEZREEL VALLEY

To the north in the **Jezreel Valley**, the gateway to the Galilee, is **Tel Megiddo** ❸ (daily 8am–4pm, until 5pm Apr–Sept), a 4,000-year-old city made famous by the Book of Revelation as the site for mankind's final battle at Armageddon. Archeologists have uncovered 20 cities including a 4,000-year-old Canaanite temple, King Solomon's stables, and an underground water system built by King Ahab 2,800 years ago. Other interesting sites to the north are **Beit She'arim** ❹ (daily 8am–4pm, until 5pm Apr–Sept), the most important Jewish burial place during the Talmudic period and **Tsipori** ❺ (daily 8am–4pm, until 5pm Apr–Sept), which includes a 500-seat Roman amphitheater, a 2nd-century mosaic of a woman dubbed "the Mona Lisa of the Galilee" and a Crusader fortress.

NAZARETH

Further east is **Nazareth** ❻, the quaint village where Jesus grew up that has become one of the world's best-known towns. Today it is a bustling city of 80,000, Israel's largest Arab city with almost two dozen churches commemorating Nazareth's most esteemed resident. The grandest of all is the monumental **Basilica of the Annunciation** (Mon–Sat 8am–6pm, until 5pm in winter, Sun 2–5pm; free). The largest church in the Middle East, it was completed in 1969, encompassing the remains of previous Byzantine churches, marking the spot where the Angel Gabriel is said to have informed the Virgin Mary that God had chosen her to bear His son.

Not your average church

The Basilica of the Annunciation has a series of elaborate murals, each from a different country - Mary appears kimono-clad and with slanted eyes; in another, she's wearing a turban and bright African garb, while the Americans have produced a highly modernistic Cubist version of the Virgin.

In the basement of the **Church of St Joseph**, which is next to the Basilica, is a cavern reputed to have been the carpentry workshop of Joseph, Jesus's earthly father. Some of the simpler churches, however, capture an air of intimacy and sanctity that the colossal Basilica lacks. This is especially so in the **Greek Orthodox Church of St Gabriel**, slightly under 1km to the north.

Mount Tabor ❼ rises to the east of Nazareth offering a panorama of the whole Jezreel Valley It was here that the biblical prophetess Deborah was said to have led an army of 10,000 Israelites to defeat their idol-worshipping enemies. Two churches commemorate the transfiguration of Christ, which is also said to have taken place here. Most notably, the Franciscan **Basilica of the Transfiguration** commemorates the event, which Christians believe foreshadowed his resurrection.

MOUNT MERON AND SAFED

North of Mount Tabor, you'll the highest peaks in the Galilee. **Mount Meron** ❽ – at 1,208 meters (3,936ft) is the highest the highest with a sweeping view from the Mediterranean to Mount Hermon is exceptional. These mountains are filled with the tombs of the rabbis such as Shimon Bar-Yochai in **Meron** village, who composed the Kabbalah, the now highly fashionable great Jewish mystical texts.

Southeast of Meron is **Safed ❾**, an attractive hilltop town where narrow, cobbled-stone streets wind their way through stone archways and overlook the domed rooftops of 16th-century houses and medieval synagogues. The rabbinical scholars of Safed were so prolific that in 1563 the city set up the first printing press in all of Asia. Not all the synagogues are medieval – many of the original ones having been destroyed and replaced by more modern structures, but the spirit of the old still lingers in these few lanes off Kikar Meginim. The special atmosphere that permeates Safed has captured the imagination of dozens of artists who have made it their home and set up an artists' colony alongside the synagogues. Towering above the center of Safed, littered with Crusader ruins, is **Citadel Hill**, an excellent lookout point, taking in the view that extends from the slopes of Lebanon to the Sea of Galilee.

THE GALILEE PANHANDLE

In the valley beneath Safed to the east is **Rosh Pina ❿**, which was first settled by Russian Jewish families in the 1880s. Cobbled-stone streets line the old section of the town, which is complete with gentrified 19th-century houses. Northwards towards Metula is some attractive countryside, the **Galilee Panhandle**, a thin

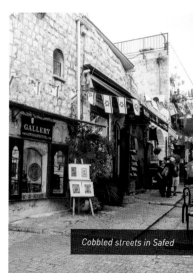

Cobbled streets in Safed

Hula Nature Reserve

strip of Israel surrounded by Lebanon and Syria. **Tel Hazor**
(daily 8am–4pm, until 5pm Apr–Sept) is one of the oldest
archeological sites in Israel – and by far the largest – with its
23 layers of civilization spanning 3,000 years.

This is the region of the **Hula Valley**, which was formerly a
malaria-infested swamp. By 1957 the lake had been emptied,
leaving a verdant valley in its place; however part of the region
has been re-swamped recently, as excessive peat in the ground
was impeding agriculture. You can get an idea of what the area
was like before the drainage by visiting the 80 hectares (200
acres) of swamp land that have been set aside as the **Hula
Nature Reserve ⑪** (Sat–Thu 8am–4pm, Fri 8am–3pm). **Metula
⑫**, Israel's most northern point and surrounded on three sides
by Lebanese land, was founded in 1896 by Baron Edmund de
Rothschild. Apart from the fresh mountain air, abundant apple

orchards and charming guesthouses, Metula offers visitors views of neighboring Lebanon.

RIVER JORDAN AND GOLAN HEIGHTS

Back to Kiryat Shmona and to the east is the archeological site of **Tel Dan** (daily 8am–4pm, until 5pm Apr–Sept), which was founded in biblical times by the tribe of Dan. Today the site features various Israelite ruins, a Roman fountain and a triple-arched Canaanite gateway. The **Dan River** provides the greatest single source of the Jordan River – in fact, "Jordan" is a contraction of the Hebrew *Yored Dan* (descending from Dan), and that's precisely what this biblical river does. For its 264km (165-mile) length, the Jordan flows from the snowy peak of **Mount Hermon** to the catchment basin of the Dead Sea, which, at 400 meters (1,300ft) below sea level, is the lowest point on the face of the earth.

Further east, the **Banias Waterfall** ⓭ is among the most popular natural attractions in the country. Roman and old Crusader ruins may also be visited at **Banias**, which is in the **Mount Hermon National Park** (daily 8am–4pm, until 5pm Apr–Sept), however the main real attraction here are the waterfalls, including the country's largest, and some inviting pools.

Banias is on the **Golan Heights**, which Israel captured from Syria in 1967, and annexed in 1981 because it had previously been used for artillery shelling of Israel. The Golan Heights is a mighty fortress created by the hand of nature. During the Tertiary Age, geological folding lifted its hard black basalt stone from the crust of the earth. Today it is a sloped plateau, rising in the north over 1,000 meters (3,280ft) high and stretches 67km (41 miles) from north to south and 25km (16 miles) from east to west.

Israeli towns and villages have been established on the Golan Heights since 1967, with parts of the windswept landscape transformed into orchards growing cherries, blackberries, raspberries and other fruits that cannot grow elsewhere in Israel, because of the heat. Domestic tourism to this region, which remains delightfully cool in the summer months, has flourished, although it remains rarely visited by overseas tourists. B&B accommodation has sprung up in most of the region's villages. The **Nimrod Fortress** ⑭ (daily 8am–4pm, until 5pm Apr–Sept) on the northern Golan Heights is 13th-century Syrian fortress, constructed to defend the waters of Banias below, one gains a spectacular view of the Northern Galilee and the Naphtali Hills beyond.

⊙ DRUZE

There are five Druze communities living on the Golan Heights with more than 20,000 inhabitants, who live peacefully within Israel but have refused to take Israeli citizenship. Many of them "pragmatically" speak publicly in support of Syria for fear that they may one day find themselves looking to Damascus as their capital. However, since the outbreak of the Syrian Civil War in 2011 that seems unlikely. Elsewhere in Israel, there are 150,000 Druze. Despite being Arabic speakers and following a religion that is an 11th-century offshoot of Islam, they maintain a determined separateness from mainstream Arab and Muslim society. Those serving in the Israeli army are often known for their bravery and commitment to the Zionist cause. Druze religious men can be distinguished by their fantastic moustaches.

MOUNT HERMON

Towering above the northern end of the Golan Heights is **Mount Hermon**  (2,814 meters/9,232ft), with several other ranges radiating from it. It occupies an area roughly 40km by 20km (24 miles by 12 miles) and is divided between Lebanon, Syria, and Israel, with several demilitarized zones under UN jurisdiction. About 20 percent of this area is under Israeli control, including the southeast ridge whose highest point rises to 2,236 meters (7,336ft). Mount Hermon's peaks are snow-covered most of the year, and Israeli ski enthusiasts have opened a modest ski resort on these slopes, with a chair-lift and an equipment rental shop for skis. The **ski resort** (open 8am–4pm generally Jan–Apr, depending on snowfall; tel: 04-698 1337) can be reached by via Majdal e-Shams.

Skiing on Mount Hermon

At the foot of Mount Hermon is **Majdal e-Shams** ⑯ is the largest of the Druze villages on the Golan Heights, and has good restaurants, and souvenir shops. The Druze village of **Mas'ada** to the south along 98 overlooks the **Ram Pool** ⑰, an extinct volcano, which over time has evolved into a small lake.

To the southwest, **Katsrin** is the "capital" of the Golan and home to the **Golan Archeological Museum** (Sun–Thu 9am–4pm, Fri 9am–1pm, Sat 10am–1pm), which exhibits artifacts from the ancient settlement of Katsrin. To the south is

Gamla 🔞 (daily 8am–4pm, until 5pm Apr–Sept), a fortified Golan town which, in AD 66, was the focus of one of the early battles in the Jewish revolt against Rome. After three full Roman legions were initially defeated, Vespasian besieged the Jewish town in one of the bloodiest battles of the war and 9,000 Jews were slaughtered or committed suicide. Today it is possible for visitors to stroll through the ancient streets of this community and inspect the remains of many ancient houses, and even a synagogue, all of which have been constructed out of the Golan's sombre black basalt stone.

Among the fields to the east of Gamla it is possible to find several prehistoric dolmens. These are Stone Age structures, which look like crude tables, with a large, flat stone bridging several supporting stones. They are generally considered to be burial monuments, and most are dated to about 4,000 BC. Dolmens are found at several other sites around the Golan and the Galilee.

SEA OF GALILEE

Glowing like an emerald, its tranquil surface framed in a purplish-brown halo of mountains, the **Sea of Galilee** 🔞 is in fact a lake of just 21km (13 miles) long and 11km (7 miles) wide. It may not be enormous by global standards, but it has, through some romantically inspired hyperbole, come to be known as a "sea". In Hebrew it is called Yam Kinneret because it's shaped like a *kinnor* or harp.

These bountiful shores have been inhabited for millennia, with the earliest evidence of habitation dating back 5,000 years to a cult of moon-worshippers that sprouted in the south. Some 3,000 years later the lake witnessed the birth and spread of Christianity on its shores, while high up on the cliffs above, Jewish rebels sought refuge from Roman soldiers. The dramas of the past, however, have since faded into the idyllic land-scape. Today it is new water sports, not new religions that are hatched on these azure shores.

It was in the fishing villages around the Sea of Galilee that Jesus found his first followers. The village of **Capernaum** , on the northern tip of the lake, became his second home. Here he is said to have preached more sermons and performed more miracles than anywhere else.

It was a metropolis of sorts in its heyday, and at least five of the disciples came from here. It is after one of them, a sim-ple fisherman named Peter, that the Galilee's most renowned fish gets its name – St Peter's fish, or *Tilapia Galilea*. Today, the village is home to the elaborate remains of a 2nd-century synagogue, built over the original one where Jesus used to

Sea of Galilee

preach. There is also a recently completed church, shaped like a ship, on the supposed site of St Peter's old house, a Franciscan Monastery and the colorful red domes roofs of the Greek Orthodox Church of the Seven Apostles.

In the neighboring town of **Ein Tabgha**, Jesus is said to have made five loaves of bread and two fishes feed the 5,000 hungry people who had come to hear him speak. The modern **Church of the Multiplication** (daily 8.30am–5pm) was constructed over the colorful mosaic floor of a Byzantine shrine in 1982. Next door is the Church of Peter's Primacy.

It was standing on a hilltop overlooking the Sea of Galilee that Jesus proclaimed to the masses that had gathered below: "Blessed are the meek, for they shall inherit the earth." This well-known line from the Sermon on the Mount is immortalized in the majestic **Church and Monastery of the Beatitudes** (daily 8am–5pm; free), an octagonal church, set in well-maintained gardens that belongs to the Franciscan order and was built in the 1930s.

TIBERIAS

The capital of the lake, **Tiberias** ㉑ is a sprawling city of 60,000, halfway down the west coast, and one of the country's most popular resorts. On its boardwalk, which is lined

Baptism at the Yardenit Baptismal Site

with seafood restaurants, you can dig into delicious St Peter's fish while enjoying stunning views of the lake. On the marina you can have your pick of water-skiing or windsurfing, or go for a dip at one of the beaches along the outskirts of the city.

Tiberias is considered one of the four holy Jewish cities (along with Jerusalem, Hebron and Safed), as it is home to the tombs of several famous Jewish sages, including the 12th-century philosopher Moses Maimonides and the self-taught scholar, Rabbi Akiva, who was killed by the Romans after the Bar-Kochba uprising. Tiberias was founded by Herod Antipas around AD 20 because of its hot springs. In the second and third centuries Jewish scholars codified the sounds of the Hebrew script and wrote the Mishnah, the great commentary on the Bible, at Tiberias.

Today, the mineral-rich **hot springs** remain a major draw. The original baths the Romans used can be seen in a fascinating **museum** (Sun–Thu 10am–noon, 3–5pm), just over the road from the **National Archeological Park**. Nearby archeologists have uncovered a 2nd-century mosaic synagogue floor and Maimonides tomb on Ben Zakai Street, just south of the hotel district, which is a popular site for Jewish pilgrims.

Baptism in the Jordan

Shortly after Jesus left Nazareth at the age of 30, he met John the Baptist preaching near the waters of the Jordan. The Bible so often describes the Jordan River as a boundary of sorts and, more figuratively, as a point of transition. It was here that Jesus was baptized. Once he was cleansed, he set out on his mission. One tradition holds that the baptism took place at the point where the Sea of Galilee merges with the Jordan River near what is today Kibbutz Kinneret, 12km (7 miles) south of Tiberias. The **Yardenit Baptismal Site** (Sat–Thu 8am–5pm, Fri

8am–4pm) has been established just outside the kibbutz in order to accommodate the many pilgrims who still converge on the spot. There is also a rival 'Site of the Baptism' further south, near Jericho. Around the point where the lake merges with the Jordan River in the south are the three oldest kibbutzim: **Dganya Alef**, **Dganya Bet** and **Kinneret 22**. Kinneret's cemetery, on the lakeside is the burial place for leading Israeli public figures and is a marvellous place for tranquil contemplation.

More ancient baths from the Roman period can be found to the east on the southern Golan Heights at **Khamat Gader 23** (Sat–Thu 9am–5pm, Fri 9am–12.30pm), near the Yarmuk River. Khamat Gader was established in the 2nd century AD by the Roman Empire's 10th Legion. Set in a secluded mountain nature reserve and with Israel's only naturally flowing hot mineral springs, this is one of the country's most popular tourist attractions. The renovated Roman baths and a range of other attractions, including treatments and massages, a water park, a crocodile farm, and other animal exhibits, are a major draw here.

BEIT SHE'AN

Southwest is the ancient archeological site, or *tel*, of **Beit She'an 24**, which reflects 6,000 years of civilization. In the **Beit She'an National Park** (daily 8am–4pm, until 8pm Apr–Sept) sits Israel's best-preserved Roman theater, which once seated 8,000; and an **archeological museum** featuring a Byzantine mosaic floor. Beit She'an was once part of the Roman Decapolis – the 10 most important cities in the Eastern Mediterranean. Also here are a colonnaded street, and a ruined temple that collapsed in an 8th century earthquake. Near the modern town of Beit She'an is the **Jordan River Crossing** border into Jordan.

Inner yard of el-Jazzar Mosque, Akko

THE MEDITERRANEAN COAST

Israel's Mediterranean coast, with its golden beaches, stretches 187km (112 miles) from the Lebanese border in the north to the Gaza crossing in the south. The best Mediterranean views are offered from atop **Mount Carmel**, which rises majestically above Haifa, the largest city in the northern region. To the north are the ancient Crusader city of **Akko** and the sea grottos at **Rosh Ha'Nikra**. To the south is the ancient Roman capital of Caesarea, Tel Aviv, and the former Philistine cities of **Ashdod** and **Ashkelon**.

Lebanese Border

Just before the Lebanese frontier, towers the rocky point of **Rosh ha-Nikra** ㉕, where a series of stunning grottoes, formed by millennia of gradual erosion, are the prime attraction. A

Cable car on Rosh Ha-Nikara

cable car (daily 8.30am–4pm, until Apr–mid-July and mid-Aug–Sept, until midnight mid-July–mid-Aug; www.rosh-hanikra.com) goes down over the pounding tide, and a footpath is also there for the determined. The cliff is the southernmost edge of the Ladder of Tyre mountain range and offers a view over the walled-up railway tunnel that once led to Lebanon. Further south is the resort of Nahariya and just north of Akko is the **Bahá'í Tomb and Gardens**, marking the burial site of Mirza Hussein Ali, the early leader of the Bahá'í faith. Surrounding the tomb is a lovely Persian garden.

AKKO

One of the world's oldest ports, **Akko** was mentioned by the Pharaohs in 1500 BC and captured by the Egyptians in 261 BC. Alexander the Great and Julius Caesar are also known to have passed through too. Akko was chosen as the key port of the Crusader Kingdom by Baldwin I in 1104, before falling to the Mamelukes in 1291. The Ottomans defeated Napoleon here in 1799, but with the establishment of a deeper port in nearby Haifa, the city sank into obscurity. In 2001, Unesco declared Old Akko a World Heritage Site.

Near the entrance to the Old City is the **visitor center** (daily 8.30am–5pm, and 6pm in summer), which is a good place to start. From here, continue to the northeastern command post, with a strategic view and a restored promenade, which continues on to Land Gate and the bay. The impressive city walls and moat were built by the Crusaders in the 12th century. In the Old City, the first prominent structure is the elegant **el-Jazzar Mosque** (open dawn to dusk), built in 1781–82, it is one of the largest mosques in the Holy Land.

Nearby is the towering **Citadel and Museum of Heroism** (Sat–Thu 9.30am–5pm, Fri 9.30am–noon). Built by el-Jazzar on Crusader ruins, the fortress has been used variously as an arsenal and a barracks and, since Turkish times, as a prison. This was where Jewish underground fighters were executed during the British Mandate. Abutting the Citadel is the dank **Subterranean Crusader City** (Sat–Thu 9am–4.30pm, Fri 9am–12.30pm). Now reclaimed, the halls are the venue for the October Akko Fringe Theater Festival, which brings together the best of Israel's experimental and alternative drama companies. As you emerge from the subterranean city, there is a restored Turkish bathhouse, which is now the **Municipal Museum** (same hours as Crusader City; tickets valid for both). The museum contains exhibits on archeology, Islamic culture, folklore, and weaponry. Wander further into Akko's maze-like streets and you'll find the Greek Orthodox **St George's Church**, dedicated to two British officers who fell at Akko in 1799 and 1840. Of special interest are the *khans* (inns) that grace the port-side area including the imposing Khan el-Afranj (Inn of the Franks) near the Bazaar, and the Khan el-Umdan (Inn of the Pillars).

HAIFA

On the gentle slopes of Mount Carmel is **Haifa** ㉗, Israel's third-largest city, a busy port with heavy industry, a high-tech

Carmelite Monastery, Haifa

center, and the Technion, the country's oldest university. The **Carmel Center** is where most of Haifa's hotels are located offering panoramic scenes of the city, sea and mountains. Atop the crest of Mount Carmel is the **University of Haifa**, with its distinctive 25-floor tower thrusting resolutely against the sky, offers an unparalleled view of northern Israel.

Near the promenade of the Carmel Center is the **Mane-Katz Museum** (Sun–Mon, Wed–Thu 10am–4pm, Tue 2–6pm, Fri 10am–1pm, Sat 10am–2pm; free), housed in the building where the expressionist artist lived in his later years. A short distance away is the **Museum of Prehistory and Haifa Zoo** (Sun–Thu 8am–3pm, Fri 8am–1pm, Sat 10am–2pm), displaying some interesting finds from the area, which date back to the time of the Neanderthal man. Continue down the slope for several kilometers for the **Carmelite Monastery** (daily 6am–1.30pm, 3–6pm), the world center of the Carmelite Order. The site was selected in the 12th century by Crusaders and the church was built in the 18th century, over a grotto associated with the prophet Elijah and his disciple Elisha. **Elijah's Cave** (Sun–Thu 8am–5pm; free) can be reached by a footpath from the monastery. The prophet is said to have meditated here in the 9th century BC, before his encounter with the Baalists on the Carmel.

Along the seafront

Opposite the monastery, a platform marks the upper terminal of Haifa's **cable car** (daily 9am–11pm, closed on Fri in winter), which ferries passengers from the Carmel down to the Bat Galim Promenade. Haifa has some glorious beaches, and because of the shape of Israel's coastline, Bat Galim beach is the only one in the whole country facing north, making it the best for surfing. Further south and slightly inland is the

⊘ BAHÁ'Í COMPLEX

Dominating the Mount Carmel hillside in Haifa, the Bahá'í Complex includes the world's longest hillside gardens, as well as the golden-domed Bahá'í Shrine and the palatial Seat of the Universal House of Justice (Bahá'í World Headquarters). The centerpiece is the gold-domed Shrine of the Báb, which contains the tomb of Siyyad Ali Muhammed – known as the Báb, a Persian Muslim who proclaimed the coming of a "Promised One" in 1844. He was executed for heresy in 1850, and his disciples brought his remains to Haifa in 1909.

Haifa became the center of Bahá'í activity when the "Promised One" – Husayn-Ali, Baha'u'llah – settled in Palestine. He is buried near Akko where he died in 1892. Baha'u'llah's son, Abbas Effendi, instructed believers to purchase large tracts of Mount Carmel overlooking Haifa Bay.

Extending from the summit of Mount Carmel, this unique hillside terraced garden, completed in 2001, spreads out spectacularly along the north-western slope of the mountain. The Shrine of the Bab and the Bahá'í Gardens are open to the public for free. Guided tours must be booked at least 24 hours in advance (tel: 04-831 3131).

Israel's only subway

The **Carmelit**, Israel's only subway, is one of a kind. Its tunnel, hacked through the interior rock of the mountain, operates on the same principle as a cable car: one train coming down from the Carmel hauls the other train up the steep incline.

German Colony, one of the most attractive parts of Haifa. Built in 1868 by the German Templar, this area has become gentrified in recent years with delightful old houses and gardens and excellent restaurants along Ben Gurion Avenue beneath the Bahá'í hillside gardens. The beauty of the German Colony has been further accentuated by the recently completed **Bahá'í Gardens** (see box), rising majestically up the hill, with the gold-domed Bahá'í shrine at their peak

THE CARMEL RANGE

South of Haifa is **Mount Carmel National Park ㉘** (open daily round the clock), Israel's largest national forest preserve with deer and gazelle roaming freely in the lush hilly woodlands. An extra fee is charged for entering the **Khai Bar Nature Reserve** (daily 8am–3pm) where rare fallow deer from Iran, previously extinct in this region, have been reintroduced.

Tucked among the slopes and valleys of the Carmel Range, are the Druze villages of **Daliyat el-Karmel ㉙** and **Isfiya**. The market places offer traditional handicrafts and pleasant cafés where Turkish coffee and succulent pastries can be enjoyed under the trees. The **Carmelite Monastery** at **Muhraka**, nearby, stands over the site where Elijah defeated the Baalists. To the south is the **Nakhal Mearot Nature Reserve ㉚** (daily 8am–4pm, until 5pm Apr–Sept), which contains caves inhabited by Neanderthals 50,000 years ago and discovered in 1929.

CENTRAL COAST

38km (22 miles) south of Haifa is **Zikhron Ya'akov** ㉛, which was established in 1882 in memory of James Rothschild. Just south of the quaint 19th century cobble-stoned city center is **Rothschild's Tomb**, built in the 1950s to house the remains of the Parisian banker and his wife Adelaide, situated amid a fragrant garden (Yad Hanadiv) of date trees, sage, roses, and other flowers.

Continuing south is **Caesarea** ㉜ (daily 8am–4pm, until 5pm Mar–Sept). Although its greatest historical importance was as a Roman colony, it is the Crusader ruins that really catch the eye here. Enter the **Crusader City** through a vaulted gatehouse and bridge over a wide moat. The walls around the city, which slope down precipitously from an imposing height, are perhaps the most awe-inspiring monument. Along the waterfront, Roman pillars were used as foundation stones by the Crusaders and jut out among the waves. There is also a Byzantine street of statues and the restored **Roman Amphitheater**, a stirring venue for concerts overlooking the Mediterranean. Inland from the ruins is one of the few golf courses in Israel.

The only remarkable thing about the city of **Khadera**, just south of

Hippodrome at Caesarea

Caesarea is its huge power station on the coast. At least the electricity company can take credit for cleaning up the River Khadera and planting an attractive parkland along its banks, south of the power station. South of Khadera is **Mikhmoret Beach**, beautiful and seldom crowded. Here you can find sandy coves to nestle in and extraordinary sunsets to gaze upon from atop the cliffs. If you are really lucky you might stumble across the local population of large sea turtles.

Several kilometers further south is **Netanya ㉝**, the capital city of the Sharon region. Founded as a citrus colony in 1929, Netanya has really blossomed since, if you'll excuse the pun. It has an attractive beach and promenade, including a striking glass elevator down to the beach just south of the city center to help the elderly and disabled negotiate the high cliffs. Netanya

Remains of the old Crusader fortress at Apollonia

has a population of 240,000 and a galaxy of budget-priced hotels clustered along the beachfront. The **Tourist Information Office** (Sun–Thu 9am–5pm) is in Independence Square near the seafront.

Just before Tel Aviv is **Herzliya** ㉞, home to many of Israel's wealthiest and a favourite with ambassadors and business executives, with stylish beaches, luxury hotels, and villas near the seafront. The most expensive part of the city, Herzliya Pituach, is between the high-tech park and the coast. On the seafront in the north of Herzliya is **Apollonia** (Tel Arshaf) in the **Sidma Ali National Park** (daily 8am–5pm; free). On this site are the ruins of an ancient Hellenistic city and a Crusader fortress.

SOUTHERN COAST

From Herzliya, the best way to bypass Tel Aviv and reach the southern coastline is, surprisingly, to drive through the very heart of the city. The Ayalon Highway (Road 20), together with a major suburban railway line, runs parallel to the sea through the city center and onto the southern suburbs of Holon and Bat Yam before reaching **Rishon Le-Tsiyon**. This city, the name of which means "First in Zion", was founded in 1882 by Polish and Russian Zionists. Rishon Le-Tsiyon is home the first synagogue built in Israel in modern times (1885), the first kindergarten to teach in Hebrew, and the first Hebrew cultural center, where the national anthem *Ha-Tikva* (The Hope) was composed and sung for the first time. Rishon Le-Tsiyon has expanded westwards and has the country's largest shopping malls and some fine beaches including **Palmakhim** immediately to the south.

PHILISTINE CITIES

Still on the coast, some 10km (6 miles) south, is **Ashdod** ㉟ with its concrete skyline. With its Philistine history now long behind it, Ashdod has become Israel's most important deep-water port. An unremarkable modern city, Ashdod's saving grace is its golden Mediterranean beaches. Outside the city, to the southeast, lies the grave of the ancient metropolis, **Tel Ashdod**. Little remains here other than a hillock and the scattered shards of Philistine pottery.

One of Israel's finest beaches is **Nitsanim**, 7km (4 miles) to the south of Ashdod, with delightful freshwater pools just inland. From here you can see the city of **Ashkelon ㊱**. Most of the Ashkelon's antiquities are within the **National Park** (daily 8am–9pm), near the seafront. Here are ruins of Herodian colonnades and ancient synagogues, a Roman avenue presided with a headless statue of Nike, goddess of victory, in a long-abandoned Roman amphitheater. The site is surrounded by a grass-covered Crusader wall.

From here it is nearly 17km (9 miles) south to the **Erez Checkpoint**, the northern frontier crossing to the Gaza Strip, the scene of so many bloody encounters between the Palestinians and Israelis.

THE SOUTH

Israel's south is predominately made up of sparsely populated desert with spectacular landscapes. The Dead Sea is the lowest point on earth with highly-salty water allowing bathers to float; the Negev Desert includes the Ramon Crater, the world's largest erosion crater created 220 million years ago; and Eilat is located on the Red Sea and is the closest tropical water resort to Europe with guaranteed year-round warm weather.

Before heading south on Highway 6 near the airport, several locations south of Tel Aviv deserve a detour. Three important mosques are in **Ramla ㊲** near the airport: the

Bell-shaped cave at Maresha

8th-century **White Mosque**; the **Mosque of the Forty**, built by the Mamelukes in 1318; and the **Great Mosque** (Sun–Thu 8–11am), situated west of the bus station near the market and built on the site of the Crusader Cathedral of St John. The **Vaulted Pool**, an underground cistern in the town's center, dates back to the 9th century. East of the airport just off Highway 1 is **Mini Israel**, with miniature models of the country's principal sites (open daily 10am–5pm, closes 2pm Fri; July, Aug open 5pm–10pm). Nearby is the French Trappist **Monastery of Latrun**, which includes the remains of a 12th-century Crusader fortress called **Le Toron des Chevaliers**. An almost perfectly preserved Roman villa and bathhouse are also located nearby.

Near Kiryat Gat is the ancient site of **Beit Guvrin** ❸❽. There are many Crusader ruins here but it is the **Maresha Caves** (daily 8am–4pm, until 5pm Apr–Sept) that are of special note

Floating in the Dead Sea

including burial caves and bell-shaped caves formed by Roman quarrying, although some date right back to Greek and even Phoenician times.

DEAD SEA

405 meters (1,300ft) below sea level, is the **Dead Sea** , the lowest point on earth, which is surrounded by the starkest scenery the world has to offer. The northern part of the Dead Sea can be reached along Highway 1 from Jerusalem while the southern part can be accessed south along Highway 6, and then cutting east to Dimona.

The Dead Sea is slowly evaporating due to overuse of the River Jordan's waters and mineral mining. The sea has already separated into two lakes, although it will be many thousands of years yet until the Dead Sea completely disappears, should it continue disappearing at the rate it is today. The road east from Jerusalem descends through the Judean Desert, a barren, billowing landscape and to the north near the Dead Sea itself is the ancient city of **Jericho**, a desert oasis now inside the Palestinian Authority.

The first northern opportunity to 'float' in the Dead Sea is at **Kalya Beach** (daily 8am–sunset) on the northwest shore. Further south is **Kumran** (daily 8am–4pm, until 5pm Apr–Sept), where the Dead Sea Scrolls were found. The Essenes, an ascetic Jewish sect of the Second Temple period, deliberately built their community in this inaccessible spot. The **Ein Fashkha** (daily 8am–4pm, until 5pm Mar–Sept) is another popular bathing site, although only in the fresh water pools. The Dead Sea's evaporation means that there is no longer safe access to the sea itself, which is surrounded by quicksand.

Further south is the **Ein Gedi Nature Reserve** ❹ (daily 8am–4pm, until 5pm Apr–Sept). The most popular hiking and bathing site in the reserve is **David's Spring**, which leads up to a beautiful waterfall, fringed in ferns. According to legend, David hid here from King Saul, when he was the victim of one of the king's rages. **Nakhal Arugot**, nearby and to the south, is a canyon full of wildlife and deep pools for bathing. **Kibbutz Ein Gedi** runs a guesthouse and a spa for bathing in the Dead Sea water and nearby sulphur springs and mud baths. A camping site, and an additional youth hostel and restaurant are situated on the shore below the kibbutz near the Ein Gedi spa. The beach is currently closed due to dangerous sinkholes.

MASADA

20km (12 miles) south is **Masada** ❹ (daily 8am–4pm, until 5pm Apr–Sept), another of Israel's spectacular archeological sites. Cut off by steep canyons on all sides, it was on this desolate mesa, in 43 BC, that Herod seized an existing fortress and built a magnificent three-tiered palace that extends down the northern cliff. The lavish palace boasted a Roman bathhouse, complete with ingenious heating system, fine mosaics, huge water cisterns carved into the rock, and of course a remarkable desert view from the summit. Masada can be climbed easily from the west via the Roman ramp, ascended by cable car from the east, or climbed via the Snake Path, also from the east. Most impressive of all is the story of the epic siege of the

Dead Sea Mud

Ein Bokek, a popular tourist enclave on the western shore of the Dead Sea, attracts health-seekers, with many hotels built around the mineral springs. The healing waters are used to treat many ailments, from skin diseases to lumbago, arthritis, and rheumatism. Hotels offer sulphur, mineral, and mud baths. Be sure to try a Dead Sea mud treatment: Cleopatra is said to have used the mud here to enhance her complexion. Today, it is exported as a natural moisturizer.

fortress: in AD 66, Jewish rebels seized Masada from its Roman garrison, an event that -triggered the Jewish War against Rome. It was only in AD 73 that the Romans finally retook Masada, with 1,000 rebels committing suicide rather than being caught.

THE NEGEV DESERT

Covering more than half of Israel, in the form of an inverted triangle, the **Negev Desert** is the only area of densely populated Israel with wide-open spaces. **Be'er Sheva** ㊸, the capital of the region is an unremarkable university town, where Abraham is said to have pitched his tent in Biblical times. Worth visiting are the **Bedouin market** to the south of the town on Thursday mornings and the city's museums in the Ottoman built old town center.

To the south is **Tel Be'er Sheva National Park** ㊹ (daily 8am–4pm, until 5pm Apr–Sept). Tel Be'er Sheva was recognized in 2005 as a Unesco Heritage Site. The site sits near the confluence of the Be'er Sheva and Hebron rivers, where settled land meets the desert. Archeologists working at Tel Be'er Sheva have uncovered two-thirds of a settlement from the early Israelite period, dating back to the 10th century BC.

65km (40 miles) further south are several Nabatean villages of major interest: **Shivta**, **Ovdat**, **Mamshit** and **Khalutsa** form a Unesco Heritage Site, called the incense or spice route. The Nabateans dominated the Negev and Edom in the first centuries BC and AD and are best known for their capital Petra in neighboring Jordan. Shivta, near the Egyptian border, is still relatively well-preserved, with three churches, a wine press and several public areas still intact.

MITSPE RAMON

An hour south of Be'er Sheva is the town of **Mitspe Ramon** ⑮, perched 1,000 meters (3,280ft) high along the northern edge of the **Makhtesh Ramon**, the largest of the three craters in the Negev, at 40km (25 miles) long and 12km (7 miles) wide. Despite its vast size, the crater comes into view quite suddenly – and it's an awesome sight when it does. Finds here include fossilized plants and preserved dinosaur footprints, dating back 200 million years to the Triassic and Jurassic periods. Mitspe Ramon has an observatory, connected with Tel Aviv University, which takes full advantage of the dry desert air. In the Makhtesh Ramon, a geological trail displays the

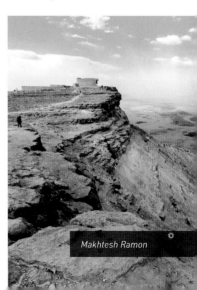

Makhtesh Ramon

melting pot of minerals that are present in the area, evident from the patches of yellow, purple and green that tint the landscape. Start off at the **Mitspe Ramon Visitors' Center** (open Sun–Thu 8am–4 pm Apr–Sept 5pm, Fri 8am–4pm; tel 08-658 8691) at the edge of town, which not only explains about the crater's unique geological formations, but also offers a splendid view.

EILAT

Eilat 46 is a hedonistic playground, a birdwatcher's delight and a crossing point for visits to Jordan and to the Sinai in Egypt. This Red Sea resort has guaranteed year-round sunshine – average January temperatures of 70°F (21°C) – the closest tropical waters to Europe. It also has remarkable marine life and coral formations, and the unique flora and fauna of the only land link between Africa and Europe and Asia. Consequently Eilat is one of Israel's most popular tourist resorts. Holidaymakers migrate instinctively, like the billion birds that fly overhead twice each year, journeying back and forth between Africa and Europe. Eilat is also a VAT-free zone, making most items here 17% cheaper than elsewhere in Israel.

The best beach is the **North Beach**, near the main hotel district. However, those wanting something more secluded might prefer the **Coral Beach Nature Reserve** (daily 9am–5pm) to the south of the city past the port. This reserve includes a fine sandy beach and a truly spectacular coral reef. Nearby are several free beaches.

The best place to see and understand the remarkable marine life is south of the city near the **Coral Beach at the Underwater Observatory Marine Park** (Sat–Thu 8.30am–5pm, Fri 8.30am–4pm; www.coralworld.com), which exhibits the Red Sea's fish of all shapes and sizes , together with coral

formations. Other options for seeing the underwater marine life include snorkeling on any of the city's beaches, hiring a glass-bottom boat, and, for the more adventurous – diving. The Red Sea coast is one of the world's great destinations for diving and Eilat, with its many government-licensed diving schools and sheltered coastline, is an ideal place to learn how to dive. Alternatively, near the port there is **Dolphin Reef** (Sun–Thu 9am–5pm, Fri–Sat until 4.30pm; www.dolphinreef.co.il), a private beach where you can swim with the dolphins.

Eilat Ornithological Park ❹ (open daily, dawn until dusk) is a five-minute drive due north of the city. It is the best place to see the millions of birds that migrate along the Great Rift Valley each year and stop here for water. Migration season begins mid-February and lasts until the end of May.

Other attractions north of Eilat include the **Khai Bar Nature Reserve** ❹ (Sun–Thu 8.30am–5pm Fri–Sat 8.30am–4pm; buy tickets at the Visitor Center) where conservationists have imported and bred a variety of animals mentioned in the Bible, which had become extinct locally including, wild asses, ostriches and numerous varieties of gazelle. The reserve is 48km (30 miles) north of Eilat near the new Ramon Airport.

Tropical waters
off Eilat

WHAT TO DO

SPORTS

PARTICIPANT SPORTS

Israel is a great place for sports enthusiasts, with excellent facilities and the opportunity to combine activities such as diving, horse riding, tennis, golf, swimming, and skiing with a general tour of the country. The Mediterranean climate means that most outdoor sports are available year round, with the exception being skiing, which is available only in winter.

The Mediterranean shoreline, the Sea of Galilee and the Red Sea are ideal for water sports, including swimming, surfing, sailing and water skiing. The marinas in Tel Aviv, Herzliya, Eilat, Ashkelon and Ashdod offer yachting as well as sailing. All the large hotels have swimming pools, and there are municipal or private pools all over the country. Many hotels have tennis and squash courts. Skin and aqualung diving are especially popular along the Gulf of Eilat; centers at Eilat will rent equipment to those with a valid international license or provide instruction for those without.

There is a fine 18-hole golf course at Caesarea and a 9-hole course north of Herzliya, at Gaash. You can also find horse-riding clubs throughout the country. Bicycles including electric-bicycles can be rented in most cities, and cycling tours of the country can easily be arranged. Electric scooters can be rented in Tel Aviv. During the winter, you can ski on the slopes of Mount Hermon.

SPECTATOR SPORTS

Soccer is the number one spectator sport in Israel, with several matches every week. Israeli teams participate in the major European competitions (the Champions League and the UEFA League). Basketball is also very popular, and Israelis are especially proud of the Maccabi Tel Aviv basketball team, which has won the European championship many times. There are many international matches during the winter season at stadiums in the Tel Aviv area.

DIVING

Israel is truly a diver's paradise. Its mild climate ensures year-round diving in the crystal-clear waters of both the Mediterranean and Red Seas, where hundreds of miles of easily accessible coral reefs and spectacular seascapes await diving enthusiasts. A variety of diving experiences are available, including underwater photography, archeological diving, grotto and cave diving. It should be noted that, unless divers have a two-star license, they must take a special diving course, though diving without a license can be done if you are accompanied by instructors.

Skin and Scuba Diving Courses

The courses for beginners last about five days and cover the theory of diving, lifesaving, physiology, physics, and underwater safety. The only conditions required to start are the ability to swim, a certificate from a doctor confirming fitness to learn diving, and a chest X-ray. Beginners can also go out on individual introductory dives, lasting from 60–90 minutes, accompanied throughout by an instructor.

It is possible to rent all the necessary skin and scuba diving equipment from **Aqua Sport** (www.aqua-sport.com) and **Red Sea Lucky Divers** (www.luckydivers.com), both in Eilat; or **Octopus Diving Center** in Tel Aviv (www.octopus.co.il).

Old City market, Jerusalem

SHOPPING

Shops tend to open long hours, usually from 9am–9pm, often even later on Saturday nights. Many shops are closed Friday afternoons and Saturday during the day for Sabbath and on Jewish holidays. Prices can fluctuate according to exchange rates but generally with the Israeli shekel very strong clothes and consumer goods are expensive – typically more expensive than in Western Europe.

For the most part, shoppers will be hunting for items that are either good value in Israel or unique to Israel including exclusive jewelry and diamonds; oriental carpets, antiquities and antiques; leather goods; paintings and sculptures; ceramics; silverware and copperware; embroidery and batiks, and of course religious requisites, particularly Judaica. Try the G.R.A.S. chain (https://www.gras.co.il/en/), with 40 stores

Rugs made from kilim pieces, Jaffa flea market

around Israel, for good value jewelry and arts and crafts gifts. For books try the nationwide Steimatzky chain.

Markets Colorful oriental markets and bazaars can be found in the narrow alleyways of the old cities of Jerusalem, Bethlehem, Akko, and Nazareth, and in Druze villages like Daliyat el-Karmel, near Haifa. These sell handmade arts and crafts, including olive wood, mother-of-pearl, leather, and bamboo items, hand-blown glass, brassware, carvings and fabrics and clothing. Be prepared to barter or you'll pay well over the odds. Jerusalem's Makhanei Yehuda and Tel Aviv's Carmel Market are great for foodies. Other popular shopping places include the weekly Bedouin market in Be'er Sheva on Thursday mornings and Nakhalat Binyamin in Tel Aviv, where artisans trade their wares on Tuesdays and Fridays.

Judaica Israel is home to a unique variety of traditional crafts, ranging from religious articles like Menorahs and mezuzot to spice boxes and wall hangings. They range from loving reproductions to stark minimalism. Centers for buying such fine crafts include several locations in Jerusalem, among them the House of Quality, Khutsot ha-Yoster (Arts and Crafts Lane), and the Me'a She'arim area. Try the latter for the best bargains while King David Street is home to the exclusive, high-end antique and Judaica stores.

VAT (sales tax) VAT (presently 17%) on purchases of more than $50 can be claimed back at Ben Gurion International Airport, on presentation of a tax receipt. After your passport has been stamped by customs, apply to the bank in the airport departure hall for a 17% refund. The following items are not included in this scheme: tobacco products, electrical appliances and accessories, cameras, film and photographic equipment. Eilat is a VAT-free zone, and VAT regulations do not apply to goods purchased there, making things 17% cheaper than elsewhere in the country. Also, many hotels and stores will exempt you from VAT, if you pay in foreign currency and present a valid passport.

Export of antiquities It is forbidden to export antiquities from Israel unless a written export permit has been obtained from the Department of Antiquities and Museums. This applies also to antiquities which accompany tourists who are leaving the country. Antiquities proved to have been imported to Israel after 1900 are exempted; for this purpose, antiquities are defined as objects made before 1700. A 10% export fee is payable on the purchase price of every item approved for export. Contact the Department of Antiquities and Museums, Rockefeller Museum, opposite Herod's Gate, POB 586, Jerusalem, for more information. It is advisable to telephone (02) 627 8627 in advance for an appointment.

ENTERTAINMENT

ARTS

Israel has a wealth of cultural and artistic entertainments. Ticket agencies in each city or town sell tickets for concerts, plays and other events. Annual festivals of all art, cultural and musical events are booked up well in advance. Calendars of Events are available at the tourist information offices. For tickets for all events, try Eventim Live Entertainment (www. eventim.co.il)

MUSIC

Israel has several orchestras, of which the most famous is the Israel Philharmonic, playing under the baton of the great conductors of the world and featuring distinguished guest artists. The Jerusalem Symphony Orchestra give weekly concerts in Jerusalem during the winter season; there are frequent performances by the Haifa Symphony Orchestra, the Rishon Le-Tsiyon Symphony Orchestra and the New Israel Opera elsewhere in the country.

THEATER

Theater is very popular in Israel, and there are many companies performing a wide range of classical and contemporary plays in Hebrew, including original works by Israelis (simultaneous translations often available). The best known are the Ha-Bima and Carmeri Theater in Tel Aviv and the Haifa Municipal Theater, which take their productions all over the country. In Jerusalem, the Center for Performing Arts includes the Jerusalem Theater, the Henry Crown Auditorium and the Rebecca Crown Theater. The Sultan's Pool Ampitheater, located beneath the walls of the Old City, is a great spot for a concert. Smaller companies offer stage productions in English, Yiddish and other languages.

MOVIES

There are multiplex cinemas in all Israel's major cities and for about $10 you can see the latest Hollywood offerings. You'll

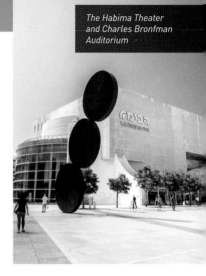

The Habima Theater and Charles Bronfman Auditorium

also find the latest movies from France, Germany and elsewhere, usually with English subtitles – ask at the box office first if unsure. Israel itself produces a dozen or so films a year, and these offer an insight into the local culture. These, too, have English subtitles. Local cinemas show golden oldies too, as well the more recent movies.

MUSEUMS

Israel has more than 100 museums. Jerusalem's Israel Museum is the national museum and a leading showcase for the country's art, archeology and Judaica. The museum's most famous exhibit is the Shrine of the Book, which displays the Dead Sea Scrolls. These scraps of tattered parchment represent the oldest known copy of the Old Testament. The Second Temple Model of Jerusalem in AD 66 is now in the Museum compound. Also in Jeruslame is the Yad Vashem Holocaust History Museum (see page 45), a striking memorial to the 6 million Jews murdered by Nazi Germany. Daring in its design, the museum is housed in a linear, triangular structure, which stretches for 160 meters (525 ft) beneath the Jerusalem hillside. The Tower of David Museum of the History of Jerusalem (see page 30), inside the body of the Citadel, contains displays describing the tumultuous history of the city.

In Tel Aviv, you'll find the Museum of the Jewish Diaspora (Bet Hatefusoth; see page 47), located on the university campus. When the museum opened in 1979, it was a radical departure from the accepted concept of a museum, as it contained no preserved artifacts. Its principal aim is reconstruction: the body of the main exhibit is handled thematically, focusing on general themes of Jewish Life in the Diaspora –family life, community, religion, culture, and the return to Zion. The Tel Aviv Museum of Art (see page 52), has four central galleries with exhibitions of 17th-century Dutch and Flemish masters, 18th-century Italian paintings, Impressionists, post-Impressionists, and a good selection of 20th-century art from the US and Europe, and modern Israeli work.

Partying on the beach, Tel Aviv

ART GALLERIES

The area around Gordon Street in Tel Aviv between Ben Yehuda and Dizengoff Streets is full of art galleries. In Tel Aviv, you can walk around the galleries at night as if they are public museums. This is acceptable behaviour and casual visitors will not be approached by eager sales staff. Another popular area with many art galleries is in Old Jaffa, near the Franciscan church.

NIGHTLIFE

Nightlife starts late in Israel and is very vibrant. From 11pm onwards, Israelis are out on the streets of Tel Aviv, and also in Jerusalem and virtually every Israeli city. Street-side cafés and restaurants are busy until well after midnight, and bars and discos have a brisk trade right through the night. In Israel, the weekend runs from Friday to Saturday, so Thursday night is the big night out.

Tel Aviv seafront and other hotspots are crowded right through the night. Nightclubs abound in the main cities and resort towns. Rock, jazz, folk and pop music are the usual fare for live music. Jerusalem and Tel Aviv are the hot spots. Bohemian Florentin is another popular nightspot in Tel Aviv, as well as the newly renovated Tel Aviv Port and Old Yafo Port.

Although not as well-known as Tel Aviv's, Jerusalem's nightlife is certainly vibrant. This is especially true between April and October, when it is warm enough to stroll through the streets and sit outside at cafés and restaurants. The city's nightlife, as elsewhere in Israel, really gets going after 10pm and the streets remain packed until well after midnight. The focus of nightlife is the Mahane Yehuda market and surrounding streets, the Russian Compound, and eastern end of Jaffa Road.

CHILDREN'S ACTIVITIES

The Israel Museum in Jerusalem has a dedicated children's wing (see page 43), whilst the hands-on Bloomfield Science Museum (see page 44) was designed with children in mind. The Israel Opera in Tel Aviv holds special weekly opera performances for children (http://www.israel-opera.co.il/eng/); whilst kids are all but guaranteed to love the world's largest miniature model park at Mini Israel (see page 77).

The Jerusalem Biblical Zoo is another must-see for children. At the Underwater Observatory Marine Park, in Eilat, children can see the wondrous marine life of the Red Sea (see page 82).

⊘ BEACHES

Israel's beaches are great fun for adults and children alike. Mediterranean beaches have golden sands but watch out for the strong undercurrent in the sea. Tel Aviv has a segregated beach near Tel Aviv Port for religious bathers although unaccompanied women often prefer this beach to prevent unwanted attention from male bathers.

There are several beaches around the Sea of Galilee, most of which charge an entrance fee. This also applies to the Dead Sea, where bathers can float due to the highly saline waters. Most of the Red Sea beaches are free and it is well worth hiring a snorkel so you can see the amazing marine life.

Israel's latitude is far south, so remember the sun can be lethal. Apply sunscreen, drink water and preferably bathe in the early morning and late afternoon.

CALENDAR OF EVENTS

January/ February: January 6 Orthodox Christmas; January 13 Armenian Orthodox Christmas.

March/ April: Purim – Celebrating the saving of Persian Jews. Traditionally Jews wear fancy dress .Passover – Seven-day festival celebrating the Exodus from Egypt. The first and last are public holidays; Jews abstain from bread throughout. Easter – Often celebrated the weekend after Passover.

May/ June: Independence Day – Marks Israel's Declaration of Independence in 1948. A public holiday. Shavuot (Pentecost) – 50 days after Passover this festival, which is also a public holiday, marks the giving of the Torah to Moses and is also a harvest festival.

July/ August: Tisha B'Av – Fast day to commemorate the destruction of both Temples. Places of entertainment are closed.

September/ October: Rosh Hashana – Jewish New Year.
Yom Kippur – Fast day. Public holiday and no vehicles travel on the roads. Sukkot – Jews build tabernacles or temporary structures to remind themselves of their 40 years in the desert after leaving Egypt during this 8-day holiday, the first and last of which are public holidays. The last day – Simchat Torah – marks the beginning and end of the annual Torah reading cycle.

November/ December: Hanukkah – The 8-day festival of lights recalls the Jewish victory over the Greeks. Christmas – The Catholic, Protestant churches celebrate the birth of Christ. The most important Muslim holidays are: Id el Adha, Sacrificial Festival. New Year; Mohammed's Birthday; Feast of Ramadan (one month of fasting from sunrise to sunset); Id el Fitr, Conclusion of Ramadan.

EATING OUT

Eating is a national pastime in Israel, one engaged in as much and as often as possible. On the street, at the beach, in every public place and in every home, day and night, you'll find Israelis tucking into food, making the country a paradise for foodies.

The biblical residents of the Land of Canaan were nourished by the fertility and abundance of a land "flowing with milk and honey." But the milk was mainly from sheep and goats, and the honey from dates, figs and carobs. Much depended on the sun, the rains and the season. Food was simple; feast predictably followed famine. Times have changed – at least in the culinary sense.

⊘ VEGAN PARADISE

Israel has emerged in recent years as one of the world's major centers of vegan cuisine (abstaining from meat, dairy and eggs). Few cities have more vegan restaurants than Tel Aviv and many eateries have vegan options – the city has an estimated 400 vegan or vegan-friendly restaurants. As kosher food separates meat and dairy, vegans feel more comfortable in a meat restaurant where dishes without meat can be guaranteed not to have any dairy items.

Perhaps most crucially the local Middle Eastern fare has traditionally been very creative with plant-based foods and the mezze savoury salads served at the start of the meal (hummus, falafel etc) is completely vegan.

Shakshuka, a typical Middle Eastern dish

Just as Israel is a blend of cultures from all over the world, so its cuisine is a weave of flavors and textures, contrasts and similarities. Israeli food is a rare merging of East and West, and the results are a profusion of culinary delights, enhanced in recent years by growing affluence, while also dulled by the import of junk food.

MEDITERRANEAN/MIDDLE EASTERN FARE

Israel's predominant culinary style reflects the country's geographical location – somewhere between the Middle East and the Mediterranean. The heavier, less healthy meat dishes brought to Israel from Europe by Ashkenazi Jews have made way for the healthier, spicier foods of Sephardi Jews. Each Jewish group, whether Moroccan, Libyan, Tunisian, Yemenite, Iraqi or native-born (Sabra) Israeli, has its own special dish. Their foods are similar yet quite distinct from each other. Basic

No pork

Don't expect pork in either kosher or traditional Muslim restaurants, as both religions strictly prohibit its consumption. Seafood, while forbidden by Jewish law and permissible by Muslim, is widely available. Shrimps and calamari are the predominant varieties.

herbs and spices include cumin, fresh and dried coriander, mint, garlic, onion, turmeric, black pepper, and sometimes cardamom and fresh green chilli.

Arab food is similar and both Arab and Jewish meals begin the same way – with a variety of savoury mezze salads. Hummus – ground chickpea seasoned with *tahini* (sesame paste), lemon juice, garlic and cumin – is probably the most popular dip, spread and salad rolled into one. You'll also find the most astounding variety of aubergine salads you've ever seen: aubergine in *tahini*, fried sliced aubergine, chopped aubergine with vegetables, chopped liver-flavored aubergine, and plenty more. Assorted pickled vegetables are considered salads as well.

While the waiters may show some signs of disappointment, you can order a selection of these salads as a meal in themselves. Or you can follow them with kebab (grilled ground spiced meat), *shishlik* (grilled sliced lamb or beef with lamb fat), *seniya* (beef or lamb in *tahina* sauce), stuffed chicken or pigeon, chops or fish.

Do try the fish, particularly in the seaside areas of Tiberias, Tel Aviv, Yafo and Eilat (there are no fish in the Dead Sea). Trout, gray and red mullet, sea bass and the famous St Peter's fish (*Tilapia Galilea*) are generally served fried or grilled, sometimes accompanied by a piquant sauce. Authentic North

African restaurants will also feature *harimeh* – hot and spicy cooked fish fragrant with an appetizing blend of tomatoes, cumin and hot pepper.

If you still have room, there's dessert. In Arab restaurants this may mean *baklawa* (filo pastry sprinkled with nuts and sweet syrup) or other rich sweets, or fruit. In typical Jewish oriental restaurants it could mean crème caramel custard, chocolate mousse or an egg-white confection laced with chocolate syrup and called (for some unknown reason) Bavarian cream. Turkish coffee, or tea with fresh mint ends the meal. If you do not want sugar in your coffee, tell the waiter in advance or your drink will be liberally sweetened.

SNACKS

Snacks play a starring role in Israeli cuisine. Favourites include bagel-shaped sesame-sprinkled breads (served with *za'atar* – an oregano-based spice mixture available only in "ethnic" settings like the Old City of Jerusalem), nuts and sunflower seeds. Pizza, blintzes, waffles and burgers all come in and out of vogue.

But the ultimate Israeli snack has to be the falafel (fried chickpea balls served in pitta bread with a variety of vegetables).

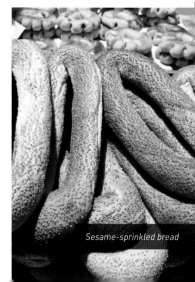

Sesame-sprinkled bread

Falafel in pitta

Along the sidewalks of major streets you can usually find several adjoining falafel stands where you're free to stuff your pitta with salads for as long as the bread holds out. Tel Aviv's Betsal'el Market is probably the most famous of the falafel centers. Located near the Carmel Market, it features an entire street of falafel vendors, with the largest salad selection this side of the Mediterranean.

FRUIT AND VEGETABLES

A trip to the open-air Makhane Yehuda in Jerusalem or the Carmel market in Tel Aviv will reveal a sumptuous array of fruit and vegetables: everything from apples to artichokes, kohlrabi to celeriac. Subtropical fruits include kiwi, mango, persimmon, loquat, passion fruit, *chirimoya* and papaya. Fresh dates, figs, pomegranates and the world's largest strawberries are among the seasonal treats. In fact, near the Carmel Market in Tel Aviv, in Kerem Hatamanim and Jerusalem's Agrippas Street by the Makhane Yehuda market can be found the best selection of restaurants.

MEAT AND MILK

If you like fowl and game, you will find chicken and turkey and, in more up-scale restaurants, goose and mullard duck (an Israeli hybrid) make excellent choices. While much beef is imported, all fowl is domestically raised.

In biblical times water was scarce and unpalatable, so milk became a major component of the diet. Goat's milk was the richest and most nourishing; next came that of sheep, then cows and finally camels. Today's Israel continues the "land of milk and honey" tradition with a wealth of familiar cheeses (camembert, brie and gouda), cottage cheese, and a wide variety of goat and sheep yogurt.

BREADS

Pita bread, with its handy pouch for tucking in meat, chips, falafel and anything edible would have brought a smile to the face of Lord Sandwich. Many restaurants will also offer *lafa*, a flatbread from Iraq made into a sandwich by wrapping it around whatever contents come to hand. In Yemeni restaurants, several types of bread are served: *mallawah* (crispy fried, fattening and delicious), *lahuh* (light, pancake-like) and *jahnoon* (slow-baked strudel-like dough). Otherwise all the standard breads are available from plain white slices to delicious French baguettes.

EATING KOSHER

The laws of *kashrut* are extremely complex, but in practical terms they mean that many animals, most notably the pig, cannot be eaten at all. Furthermore, kosher animals such as the cow and chicken must be killed in a specific way (by having their throats cut), otherwise the meat is not considered kosher. The blood must also be drained out of kosher meat, often making a steak, for example, somewhat desiccated and lacking in flavor.

In addition, while most fish are permissible, all seafood (prawns, lobsters and octopus) is considered unclean. Finally, meat and milk cannot be consumed together in the same meal.

That said, many secular Jews disregard dietary laws, and most restaurants in Israel, especially those outside Jerusalem, are not kosher. Outside of hotels, all kosher restaurants are closed on the Jewish festivals and the Sabbath – from sunset on Friday through to sunset on Saturday.

SOFT DRINKS

As in Britain, "soda" refers to soda water and not a flavored carbonated drink as it does in the US. The most delicious and healthiest drinks to try are the wide range of fruit juices. For a few dollars, street vendors will squeeze you an orange, carrot, grapefruit, kiwi or a dozen other fruits. All the usual carbonated drinks such as colas are available, in both regular and diet forms.

TEA AND COFFEE

Don't expect a good strong English tea with milk anywhere, but most restaurants give a good choice of herbal teas that are drunk without milk.

Israelis take their coffee very seriously. Most popular are Middle Eastern coffee (*botz*), Bedouin coffee (*botz* with *hell* – a spice known as cardamom in English), Turkish coffee, Viennese coffee (*café hafuch*), espresso, and filter coffee.

Turkish and Middle Eastern coffee can be very small and very strong. If you are thirsty, and not just in need of a caffeine-shot, order a glass of iced water with it. Remember to tell the waiter when you order if you don't want your coffee sugared.

ALCOHOL

Quality wines have become more popular in Israel, pushing aside the sweet red wines traditionally preferred for religious benedictions. In recent decades, Israeli wine growers have discovered that viticulture is a skill best practiced in the cooler inland hills, with state-of-the-art wineries importing knowhow and the finest vine stock from France, California, and Australia.

All wineries, big and small, are happy to show visitors around and offer wine tasting. The largest and oldest winery is

Queuing for coffee in Tel Aviv

Carmel Wines in Zikhron Yaacov. Also worth visiting is Golan Wines in Katzrin, and Barkan near Rekhovot; there are wine trails in the Upper Galilee and around Beit Shemesh in the Jerusalem Hills. There are several local beers, both bottled and draught, and a range of imported beers that real-ale specialists will probably turn up their noses up at. There are both home-distilled and imported spirits and liquors. The local specialty is *arak*, which is very similar to Greece's *ouzo*.

Although Israel has none of the alcoholic inhibitions of its Islamic neighbours, most Israeli Jews consume relatively small amounts of alcohol compared with Europeans and Americans. Excessive drinking, or even smelling of alcohol, is viewed with suspicion by society at large. Cafés and restaurants in Arab neighborhoods often do not serve alcohol.

Vineyard in Israel

TO HELP YOU ORDER

A table for....... **shulkhan le....**

1/2/3/4 **ekhad/shnayim/shlosha/arba-a**

Thank you. **Toda**

I'd like to reserve a table for two. **avakesh lehazmin shulkhan le shnayim**

May I see the menu please? **ukhal lir-ot et tafrit bevakasha**

Do you have a set menu? **yesh lakhem tafrit kavu-a**

I'd like a bottle of wine. **avakesh bakbuk yeyn**

I'd like a tea. **avakesh te**

a coffee **avakesh kafe**

a coffee with milk **avakesh kafe bekhalav**

How much longer will our food be? **kama zman od nekhake la-okhel**

The check, please. **kheshbon bevakasha**

I'd like to pay. **avakesh leshalem**

I think there's a mistake in this bill. **ani khoshev/ khoshevet sheyesh ta-ut bakheshbon**

Is service included? **ze kolel sherut**

FROM THE MENU

Bread **lechem**

Butter **chem'a**

Dessert **kinuach**

Fish **dug**

Ice cream **glida**

Meat **basar**

Milk **chalav**

Salt **melach**

Salad **salat**

Soup **marak**

Rice **orez**

Potatoes **tapuach adama**

PLACES TO EAT

Expect to pay the following for a three-course meal for one person

$$$ 250–400 shekels
$$ 100 –250 shekels
$ under 100 shekels

JERUSALEM

Abu Shukri $ *63 Al Wad Road (Via Dolorosa), tel: (02) 6271538.* Arab restaurant in the Old City that is legendary for its hummus. Open daily 8am–4.30pm later in summer and Saturdays.

Agas Vetapuach (Pear and Apple) $$ *6 Safra Square, Jerusalem, tel: (02) 623 0280*, https://www.rol.co.il/sites/eng/a-t. Excellent Italian, served food in a relaxed Jerusalem environment. Kosher. Open Sun–Thu 11am–11pm.

Al Dente $$ *50 Ussishkin Street, Jerusalem, tel: (02) 625 1479*, https://www.rol.co.il/sites/eng/al-dente/. Small neighborhood restaurant in Rehavia that offers its own unique Italian cuisine at modest prices. Kosher and non-meat menu. Sun–Thu noon–11pm, Fri 11am–4pm, Sat 8pm–midnight.

Arabesque (at the American Colony Hotel) $$$ *Nablus Road, Jerusalem, tel: (02) 627 9777*, www.americancolony.com/dining-and-events-in-jerusalem/restaurants-and-bars/the-arabesque. Á la carte menu with Middle Eastern dishes and *cordon bleu* international cooking. Open daily 6.30am–midnight.

Arcadia $$$ *10 Agripas (in the alleyway, tel: (02) 624 9138.* French cuisine with Middle-Eastern improvisations by its Iraqi Jewish chef. Kosher. Open daily 7pm–10.30pm. Friday also 8am–4pm. Reservations advisable.

Aroma $ *Mamilla Pedestrian Mal., tel: (02) 624 1304*. This new branch of a national chain of quality coffee houses provides stirring views of the Old City walls, with good value light meals and sandwiches. Kosher. Open Sun–Thu 8am–midnight, Fri 8am–4pm, Sat 8pm–midnight.

Crave Gourmet Street Food $$ *1 Hashikma Street*, http://www.facebook.com/gotcrave. Established by an American chef, the cramped eatery serves up US specialties from hamburgers and corned beef sandwiched to tortillas. Kosher. Open Sun–Thu midday–11.30pm Fri closes afternoon Sat opens after sunset.

Darna $$$ *3 Horkenos Street, tel: (02) 624 5406*, https://darna.co.il/en/. North African food with a Berber influence and Moroccan atmosphere such as authentic implements and ceremonial service. Kosher. Open Sun–Thu 7pm–11pm, Sat after sunset.

Dublin $ *4 Shammai Street, tel: (052) 836 5323*. A little piece of Ireland in Jerusalem. However be warned that late at night the emphasis is more on disco with plain Western food to go with the beer. Open daily 11am–3am.

Eucalyptus $$ *Felt alley (between 14 Hativat Yerushalayim and Dror Eliel Street), tel: (02) 624 4331*. Offers an unusual choice of local foods, served as a modern interpretation of biblical cuisine. Open Sun–Thu 5pm–11pm.

Focaccia Bar Hamoshava $$ *35 Emek Refaim, German Colony, tel: (02) 538 7182*. Good quality meat and fish grill restaurant although focaccia itself is not its forte. Kosher. Open Sun–Thu 11am–midnight Fri 8.30am–midday and Sat night.

Hummus Ben Sira $ *3 Ben Sira Street, tel: (02) 625 3893*. Kosher, delicious and very reasonably priced hummus eatery with chicken dishes, located between downtown and the Mamilla mall. Kosher. Open Sun–Thu 11am–11pm Fri 9am–4pm.

Kaffit $ *35 Emek Refaim, tel: (02) 563 5284.* Best known café in the fashionable German Colony. Kosher. Open Sun–Thu 7.30am–1am, Fri 7.30am– to Shabbat, Sat night.

La Regence, at King David Hotel. $$$ *23 Ha Melekh David, King David Hotel, tel: (02) 620 8795,* https://www.la-regence.co.il/. Le Regence is onsidered the city's finest kosher restaurant in all of Jerusalem. Nouvelle cuisine and traditional French cooking combining classical and innovative dishes. Kosher. Open Sun–Thu 7pm–10pm and Saturday after sunset.

Link $$ *3 Hama'alot Street, tel: (053) 809 4510.* Bar and bistro in downtown Jerusalem with a diverse selection of foods set in an attractive old building and courtyard. Open daily midday–11pm.

Mike's Place $ *37 Yafo Street, near Zion Square, tel: (02) 267 0965,* http://www.mikesplacebars.com/site/en/mikes-place-nightlife-jerusalem/. English-style pub with live music and live TV soccer, together with a wide choice of draft beers and hearty pub grub dishes. Open daily 11am–3am.

Notre Dame $$$ *8 Shivtei Yisra'el Street, tel: (02) 628 8018.* Situated in the magnificent Notre Dame hospice building opposite the Old City's New Gate, this is one of the city's finest restaurants but offers good value French fare. Open daily 7–11pm.

Rimon Café $$ *4 Lunz, Jerusalem, tel: (02) 625 2772.* A popular hang-out, spot located by the Ben Yehuda Street Mall, offering a choice of light meals and cakes. Kosher. Open Sun–Thu 8am–midnight, Fri 8am–3pm, Sat night.

Simas $$ *78 Agripas, Jerusalem, tel: (02) 423 3002.* Speedy service and good value food are to be found in one of the Jerusalem's best value steak eateries. Kosher. Open Sun–Thu noon–11pm, Fri noon–4pm, Sat night.

TEL AVIV

Abulafia $ *4 Yefet Street, Yafo, tel: (03) 682 8544.* Tel Aviv's best known Middle Eastern fast food restaurant, located by Jaffa's landmark clock tower, is a great spot for schwarma, falafel and hummus. Open daily 11am–3am.

Benny Hadayag $$ *Old Tel Aviv Port, tel: (053) 944 4154.* One of Israel's leading fish restaurants where you can also savour the atmosphere of Tel Aviv's recent re-invention of its Old Port as a leisure complex. Open daily midday–midnight.

Café Noir $$$ *43 Ahad Haam Street.* Not a café as the name suggests but an upmarket brasserie in an elegant setting in an old Tel Aviv building with a Viennese flavor and Mediterranean twist. Try the schnitzel. Open Sun–Thu midday–11.30pm Fri, Sat midday–midnight.

Café Nordau $ *51 Nordau Boulevard, tel: (052) 423 9383.* A trendy sidewalk café that is popular with the city's LGBTQ community. Open Sat–Thu 11am–1am Fri: 11am–6pm

Chinese Wall $$$ *26 Mikve Israel, tel: (03) 560 3974.* http://chinesewall. rest.co.il/. This Chinese restaurant is one of the city's few top quality kosher restaurants outside of the hotels. Open Sun–Thu 11am–11pm, Fri 11am–4pm, Sat night.

Meshek Barzilay $$ *6 Ahad Ha'am Street, Neve Tzedek, tel: (03) 516 6329.* One of Tel Aviv's longest-established vegan restaurants, Meshek Barzilay, is a fine example of the creativity developed by the city's vegan chefs. Open Sun 8am–4pm Mon–Thu 8am–11pm Sat 9am–11pm.

TYO $$$, *tel: (03) 930 0333.* This is perhaps Tel Aviv's finest Japanese restaurant, and is located in a lounge-bar environment set within an elegant and striking old building. Specializes in seafood. Open daily 7pm–midnight.

Zion $$ *4 Peduim, Carmel Market, tel: (03) 517 8714.* The most popular and oldest of the meat restaurants in the city's famous Yemenite Quarter (Kerem ha-Teimanim) by the Carmel Market. Kosher. Open Sun–Thu noon–midnight, Fri noon–4pm, Sat night.

Lev Harachav ("Wide Heart") $ *10 Rabbi Akiva Street, Carmel Market, tel (054) 473 6622* A no-nonsense, tasty and cheap authentic Israeli restaurant, serving excellent hummus. Kosher. Open Sun–Fri noon–1.30pm

Meat Kitchen $$$ *65 Yigal Alon Street, tel (03) 536 4755,* http://www. meatkitchen.co.il/. A chef restaurant for meat lovers with artistically presented dishes. Kosher. Open Sun–Wed midday–midnight Thu midday–1am Fri midday–5pm Sat night

Molly Bloom's Traditional Irish Pub $$ *2 Mendele Street, tel: (03) 522 1558*. One of many Irish pubs near the seafront with an authentic atmosphere, live Irish music, live sports, expensive beer, and of course, pub grub. Open Sun–Thu 4pm–2am, Fri 2pm–2am Sat 3pm–2am

Orna and Ella $$ *33 Sheinkin Street, tel: (03) 525 2085*. Started life as a café on trendy Sheinkin Street and developed into a bistro with an emphasis on homemade breads, pastries, and pastas. Open daily 10am–midnight.

Rahmo Hagadol $ *98 Derekh Menachem Begin, tel: (03) 562 1022*. The pick of Tel Aviv's hummus and falafel restaurants. Remarkably still going near the upmarket Sarona complex. Excellent, clean and astonishingly cheap. Kosher. Open Sun–Thu 9am–5pm Fri 9am–2pm.

Saluf & Sons $ *80 Nahlat Binyamin Street, tel: (03) 522 1344*. Yemenite hummus and meat restaurant, which has retained its modest atmosphere and cheap prices, despite its popularity with Tel Aviv society. Open Sun–Thu 11am–11pm Fri 10am–6pm

The Old Man and the Sea $$ *101 Retzif Ha'alyah Hashnia, Jaffa, tel: (03) 544 8820*. Middle Eastern restaurant on Jaffa port quayside serves an excellent mezze salad spread followed by grilled meats and fish. Open daily 11am–midnight

Topolopompo $$$$ *14 Hasolelim Street, tel: (03) 691 0691*, http://www.topolopompo.co.il/1858-2/. Asian fusion food in what is considered one of the finest and most expensive restaurants in the city. Open Sun–Thu midday–11pm Fri 6pm–11pm

Vong $$ *15 Rothschild Boulevard, tel: (03) 633 7171*, http://www.vong.co.il/eng. Israel's premier Vietnamese restaurant offers tasty cuisine and reasonable prices for one of Tel Aviv's most expensive addresses. Open daily midday–midnight

416 $$ *16 Ha'arba'ah Street, tel: (03) 775 5060*. New York-style vegan restaurant with quality and creative meat substitute dishes. Open daily midday–11pm

EILAT

Eddie's Hideaway $$ *2 Hamasger Street, tel: (08) 637 1137*. Eddie specializes in a range of creative meat and fish dishes. Open daily 6pm–midnight.

Ginger Asian Kitchen $$ *12 Yotam Street, tel: (08) 637 2517*. One of the city's newer restaurants offering Sushi and Asian fusion food, this restaurant is trendy but informal; it is advisable to book in advance. Open daily noon–3am.

King's Table $$$ *King Solomon's Palace Hotel, tel: (08) 638 7797*. Serves excellent Israeli breakfasts (lots of fruit, vegetables, dairy, cereals and fish but no meat), with a great view overlooking the sea. Dinner here consists of a good selection of meat and fish and as much beer as you can drink. Kosher. Open daily noon–midnight.

The Three Monkeys *Promenade by the Royal Beach Hotel, tel: (08) 636 8888*. The city's most popular English-style pub, with plenty of draught beers and hearty meals. Located on a busy promenade. Open daily 9pm–3am.

The Last Refuge $$ *Coral Beach, tel: (073) 702 7301*. South of the city, by Coral Beach, this restaurant has an excellent choice of fish and seafood. Open daily noon–midnight.

Tikka Massala $ *1 Haorgim Street Industrial Zone, tel: (08) 633 6631*. Excellent Indian restaurant, tucked away in the industrial zone north of the city. Specializes in chicken and vegetarian dishes and even offers chips on the side. Open Sun–Fri 11am–11pm

Shipudei Eilat $ *8 Kampan Street. Ice Mall, tel: (08) 633 2211*. In the Ice Mall north of the north beach, this is one of the city's best-value kosher meat eateries including Shipudei Eilat; it is also one of the few non-hotel kosher restaurants. Open Sun–Thur noon–11am Fri. 11am–4pm Sat night.

HAIFA

Dan Panorama Haifa Restaurant $$$ *107 Hanassi Avenue, Central Carmel, tel: (04) 835 2222*. Delicious buffet style Israel breakfasts and meat/fish dinners with the best view of Haifa Bay from Mount Carmel. Kosher. Open daily 7am–midday 6pm–11pm.

Douzan $$ *35 Ben Gurion Street, German Colony, tel: (054) 944 3301*. An unusual fusion of oriental and Western food with an Eastern ambience in the delightful German Colony. The Arab-owned restaurant's diverse cuisine echoes the relative ethnic and religious tolerance of the city. Open daily 11pm–midnight.

Fattoush $$ *38 Ben Gurion Street, Germany Colony, tel: (04) 852 4930*. Another excellent Arab-owned restaurant in the German Colony beneath the Bahá'í hillside gardens with an excellent array of creative Middle Eastern dishes for vegetarians and meat-eaters. Open daily 11pm–midnight.

La Terrazza $$ *46 Moriah Boulevard, tel: (04) 810 1100*. Good value Italian and Mediterranean cusine with a great view from the terrace. Open Sun–Thu noon–midnight, Fri–Sat 8pm–1am.

Shawarma Ahim Sabah $ *37 Allenby, tel: (04) 855 2188.* Located in midtown Hadar, this restuarant specialises in meat cut from the spit and eaten in pitta with a wide range of salads and relishes. Open daily 11am–midnight.

Yan Yan $$ *28 Yafo, Haifa Port, tel: (04) 866 0022.* Excellent tasting and value Vietnamese and Chinese cuisine, served in a simple setting located in Haifa's downtown port area. Open daily noon–11pm and to midnight on Fridays.

GALILEE

Dag Al Hadan $$ *Tel Dan near Kiryat Shmona, tel: (04) 695 0225.* Dine on fresh fish pulled from the River Jordan in a tranquil rural atmosphere. Speciality is trout. Open daily midday–10pm.

Decks Restaurant $$ *13 Gdud Barak Street, Tiberias, tel: (04) 671 0800.* An opportunity to eat the famous biblical St Peter's fish (*Tilapia Galilea*), whilst overlooking the Sea of Galilee. The restaurant also serves excellent steaks and a good variety of vegetarian dishes. Open daily midday–11pm.

Little Tiberias Restaurant $$ *5 Kishon Street, Tiberias, tel: (04) 679 2148.* Steakhouse and seafood restaurant with vegetarian and vegan options. Open daily midday–midnight.

A-Z TRAVEL TIPS

A SUMMARY OF PRACTICAL INFORMATION

A

ACCOMMODATIONS

There is a wide choice of accommodation in Israel, from deluxe suites in high-end hotels through to budget hotels, bed and breakfasts, youth hostels, and of course, plenty of Airbnb listings. There are also unique forms of Israeli accommodation including kibbutz guesthouses, *zimmers* (rural homes in farming communities), and Christian hospices, which exude 19th-century European ambience. Also worth looking are field schools, a national network of upmarket youth hostels.

There is a certain lack of charm about Israeli hotels, many of which offer modern comfort and convenience without much character or style. However, in recent years, quality boutique hotels have sprung up, especially in the older Tel Aviv neighborhoods and Jaffa.

Hotel rates are generally quoted in dollars and are relatively expensive – think London and New York prices. If you pay in foreign currency you are exempt from the standard 17 percent VAT, except in the VAT-free zone of Eilat.

ADMISSION CHARGES

Israel's major museums are relatively inexpensive, charging an entrance fee of about $10, with reductions available for children, senior citizens, and students. The Israel Museum charges half price for repeat visits; whilst the Yad Vashem Holocaust Museum is free. The Israel National Parks Authority, which runs the major archeological sites, charges a $6 admission fee, half price for children and senior citizens. It is well worth buying a ticket for the entire country's national parks for $25 in advance. For more details, see https://www.parks.org.il/en/article/money-saving-tickets/.

AIRPORTS

Ben Gurion International Airport is the main hub for international air traffic. It is 15km (9 miles) from Tel Aviv, and 50km (30 miles) from Jerusalem. There are two terminals: Terminal 3 for international passengers and Terminal 1 for domestic flights and international passengers on budget airlines such as easyJet, Ryanair, and Wizz Air. There is a free shuttle bus service between Terminals 1 and 3 and the car parks. The airport has several ATMs and a post office, which is open 24 hours a day (except during Shabat).

There are three other international airports in Israel: **Ramon International Airport**, recently opened and 14km (9 miles) north of the Red Sea resort of Eilat; **Sde Dov Airport**, Tel Aviv's city airport has mainly domestic flights plus a few international flights to Greece and Cyprus; and **Haifa Airport**, which has mainly domestic flights and the odd international flight to Greece and Cyrpus.

To and From Ben Gurion:

Train. There is a rail link from Terminal 3 to Jerusalem, Tel Aviv and all parts of the country except Eilat and the Upper Galilee. Details about times of trains and fares can be found at www.rail.co.il/en. There are no train services on the Jewish Sabbath, from Friday sunset to Saturday evening, or on public holidays. There are no trains after midnight and before 3am. There is a regular service to Tel Aviv, and from there, to most major cities in Israel.

Taxis. Taxis to Jerusalem cost about $50–60, and to Tel Aviv about $30–35.

Shared Taxis. This service to Jerusalem costs about $20 per person. For booking a shared taxi from your hotel or any other address in Jerusalem back to the airport, telephone Nesher: (02) 625 7227, 1 599 500 205. The service to Haifa costs about $30 – for booking back to the airport phone Amal: (04) 866 2324.

B

BICYCLE-SCOOTER HIRE

Tel Aviv alone has 90 mile (150km) of bicycle tracks including along the entire length of the seafront promenade. Most of the cities along the coast also have excellent bicycle paths. The city is home to the Tel-O-Fun bike-sharing rental scheme (https://www.tel-o-fun.co.il/en/), and the Mobike operate a bike-share scheme (www.mobike-israel.co.il). US electric scooter ridesharing company Bird also operates in Tel Aviv; electric scooter and electric bike ridesharing company Lime also plans to launch Israel operations.

BUDGETING FOR YOUR TRIP

Israel can be expensive but public transport is cheap, as are youth hostels and falafel eateries. Modest accommodations start at $50 a night and a luxury hotel may cost $150 or even more. But you can find a youth hostel for just $25 a night. Good negotiating skills can bring down prices considerably in all situations. A cheap meal in a restaurant is likely to cost $15 and a good meal with wine no more than $50. Best value is a falafel in pitta bread and as much salad and chips as you want for just $10. A flat-fare bus ticket in a city costs $2 and the bus or train between Tel Aviv and Jerusalem is about $6. The taxi between the two cities would cost $40. A cinema ticket is $10 ($15 for 3D).

C

CAR HIRE

Car hire companies require drivers to be over 21 and to have held a full license for at least one year. Drivers must present an international driving license, or national license if written in English or French, plus a passport and international credit card. Many of the world's best car hire companies have outlets with branches at the airports and around the major cities. Israel's largest car-hire company, Eldan, also has offices overseas.

Car hire costs around $250 a week for a small saloon or $350 a week for a medium-sized car. There are major extra charges for full comprehensive insurance, children's seats, which are a legal requirement, and GPS. Traffic can be heavy and parking difficult in Israel's big cities.

Hiring a car, though convenient, is not necessarily vital for the center of the country, which has good bus, rail and taxi services. Hiring a car can be the best way of touring the Galilee or the Negev. Note that car hire companies will deduct parking and police fines from your credit card plus a handling fee. Similarly, they will also take the toll charges from Highway Six and the Tel Aviv Fast Lane plus a handling fee. Payments in foreign currency are exempt from VAT.

CHILDREN

Israelis love children, who are expected to be seen and heard, and you should not feel threatened by the forward behaviour of strangers in the street or on the next restaurant table. They are likely to engage in conversation with your child and offer all types of candies.

Eating: Restaurants, hotels and cafés are very flexible in meeting children's fussy food needs, but tend not to have formal children's menus. McDonald's, Burger King, and, Pizza Hut are always on hand for children who like familiar fast food.

Accommodation: Many hotels operate baby-sitting services and are very flexible in adding beds in the parents' room for a minimal rate for an additional child. Here, too, good negotiating skills and persistence can help.

Transport: Children under 5 travel for free on buses, but thereafter pay full fare (unless they have a multi-ride ticket). On the trains, children under 5 go free and get a 20 percent discount between the ages of 5 and 10. Children under 4 must be harnessed into special seats when travelling in cars, except for taxis.

CLIMATE

For a small country Israel has very diverse climate zones. Israeli summers are long (lasting from April to October), hot and virtually rainless. During these months Tel Aviv and the coast are humid, while the atmosphere in hill towns such as Jerusalem is drier and cooler. As Jerusalem is in the hills, summer evenings can be pleasantly cool. The

	J	F	M	A	M	J	J	A	S	O	N	D
°C	12	13	15	21	25	28	30	30	30	26	17	15
°F	53	55	59	70	77	82	86	86	86	79	62	59

winter season (from November to March) is generally mild, but cold in hilly areas (close to freezing at nights). Spells of rain are interspersed with brilliant sunshine. During the winter the Tiberias area on the Sea of Galilee, the Dead Sea and Eilat (all very hot during summer) have ideal warm, sunny weather.

The weather allows for year-round bathing. From April to October, along the Mediterranean coast and around the Sea of Galilee; conditions are perfect. Throughout the year, though especially enjoyable in winter, the Dead Sea shore and the Gulf of Eilat are great spots to soak up some sun. All rain falls between October and April, with most of it concentrated in December, January and February.

What to Wear. Dress in Israel is informal by Western standards. Few people wear jackets and ties in the summer except for business occasions. However, even in the summer, Jerusalem can get quite cool in the evenings. Be sure to bring some conservative clothes for visiting religious sites. It is recommended to keep arms, legs and shoulders covered to prevent sunburn. Also, wear a hat for sun protection.

CRIME AND SAFETY

Israel has a high rate of non-violent crimes (theft from homes, cars, and pick-pocketing) but relatively little violent crime (mugging, murder, and rape). Do not leave valuables in hotel rooms, or cars, or leave wallets sticking out of pockets. In terms of violent crime, the security situation is the most pressing problem, but incidents are few and far between. Do not leave unattended baggage in public places – police sappers may blow them up. Report all suspicious packages. Before visiting the West Bank or Gaza, enquire about the current security situation. For the police, call 100 (emergencies) or 110 (information).

Marijuana/cannabis is illegal in Israel, but prosecutions are rarely brought. However, tourists should act with caution. Medical cannabis is legal and this has swamped the market with high-quality locally grown cannabis.

CUSTOMS REGULATIONS

The EU-style red–green customs clearance system is in operation at Israeli airports. Tourists with nothing to declare may choose the Green Channel and leave the airport. Tourists bringing in very expensive equipment (for example large cameras), even if exempt from duty, must use the Red Channel.

Every adult tourist may bring into the country, without payment of duty: aftershave or perfume not exceeding 0.2 liters, wine up to 2 liters and other alcoholic drinks not exceeding 1 liter; tobacco or cigars not exceeding 250 grams or 250 cigarettes; gifts up to $200, including food not exceeding 3kg (6.5lb), on the condition that no single type of food exceeds 1kg (2.2lb).

Portable, expensive electronic items such as cameras, video cameras and laptop computers may also be taken into the country duty-free, so long as they are taken out on departure. Two laptops are allowed, if one is for personal use and one for professional use. Few checks are made these days on compact, inconspicuous items.

The customs authorities are entitled to demand deposits on any article brought in by a tourist or sent separately. This is enforced only for very expensive professional equipment. Deposits are returned when leaving Israel with the article. For further information, see https://taxes.gov.il/English/customs/Pages/TaxesCustomsLobby.aspx

D

DISABLED TRAVELERS

For a list of tourist services for the disabled contact Yad Sarah at Yad

Sarah House, Kiryat Weinberg, 124 Herzl Boulevard, Jerusalem 96187; tel: (02) 644 444; www.yadsarah.org. The website lists museums and other places that are accessible for those in wheelchairs.

DRIVING

Israelis drive on the right with much horn-honking, overtaking on the inside, and weaving in and out traffic. In rural areas, roads are much quieter. With well over 3.5 million vehicles on the roads, Israel has one of the world's most densely populated road systems. There are around 350 fatalities each year from road accidents, comparable with death rates on Western European roads.

Laws are strictly enforced. Seat belts must be worn at all times (front and back) and children under the age of four strapped into appropriate seats. Speed limits are 90–120kmh (55–68mph) on highways and 50–70kmh (30–40mph) in urban areas. There are many speed and traffic light cameras on highways with fines of up to $250 for exceeding the speed limit by more than 10 percent, or crossing a red light.

Using a phone not in a hands-free installation is an offence, which police can penalize with a $250 fine. Drink-driving laws are strictly enforced. Israelis tend to move off very quickly at traffic lights the moment they turn green, making it especially dangerous to shoot a red light even before the one-second grace that the police give drivers before issuing a ticket.

Fuel is about the same price as Western Europe. In Eilat, a VAT-free zone, you do not pay the 17 percent VAT charge on fuel.

Parking is difficult in city centers and it is best to look for a parking lot. If a curb is marked blue and white, you can pay by downloading an app: Pango www.pango.co.il or Cellopark www.cellopark.co.il. If you don't pay, you are liable for a $30 fine. Do not ignore red and white marked curbs or No Parking signs. If you park here you may be clamped, or even towed away.

Toll roads There is a toll for Highway Six, which is collected electronically on the central and northern sections. Car hire firms charge a handling fee for using Highway Six. In the Carmel Tunnels, a small fee is collected at toll booths. The Tel Aviv Fast Lane costs from $2 to $30 depending on how badly jammed the highway and there is an extra handling fee for vehicles not registered in advance. The toll is clearly marked at the entrance to the lane. Vehicles with four passengers including the driver travel free but you must register with an inspector half way along. It is also possible to pay the toll to the inspector and avoid handling fees, especially with a rented car. There is also a free park-and-ride service in the lane with buses to Tel Aviv's Azrieli Center and Ramat Gan's Diamond Exchange.

E

ELECTRICITY

Standard voltage in Israel is 220 volts AC (single phase 50 cycles). Most plugs are three-pin but in some instances can be two-pin. Adaptors and transformers can be purchased throughout Israel.

EMBASSIES

Jerusalem
UK Consulate
Bet Ha'Omot Building, 101 Hebron Road, 1st Floor, West Jerusalem.
Tel: (02) 671 7724.
US Embassy & Consulate General
14 David Flusser Street
Tel: (02) 630 4000
Tel Aviv
Australian Embassy
23 Yehuda Halevy Street
Tel: (03) 695 5000
www.australianembassy.org.il
Canadian Embassy
3 Nirim Street, 63405.

Tel: (03) 636 3300.
Visa section, 7 Khavakuk ha-Navi.
www.dfait.-maeic.gc.ca/telaviv
Embassy of the Republic of South Africa
12 Abba Hillel Street, Ramat Gan
Tel: (03) 525 2566.
Ireland
2 Jabotinsky Street, Ramat Gan
Tel: (03) 696 4166.
UK Embassy
Tel: (03) 7251222
Consular Section, 1 Ben Yehuda.
US Embassy Branch Office
71 Ha-Yarkon,Tel Aviv 63903.
Tel: (03) 519 7575.

EMERGENCIES

In case of a serious accident or emergency, telephone for an ambulance
101 and/or police 100; the fire service is 102.

G

GETTING THERE

The most popular way to get to Israel is to fly. For more information,
see Airports (page 115). Few visitors to Israel arrive by land, however
there are land crossings from Egypt at Taba (near Eilat) and from
Jordan (near Eilat, the Allenby Bridge and near Beit Shean). Some
cruise ships call in at Haifa and Ashdod ports. For information on how
to get around in Israel, see Public Transport (page 126).

GOVERNMENT

Israel is a democracy with a 120-member single chamber Knesset (parliament), elected every four years by all citizens aged 18 and over. Seats

are allocated by proportional representation. The president, elected every five years by a secret ballot of Knesset members, is a titular head of state, like the British monarch. After elections the president asks the leader of the largest party to become prime minister and form a government. The Supreme Court has the power to interpret Knesset legislation.

GUIDES AND TOURS

So much history gets missed without an expert guide to explain the significance of each site, so it is well worth joining an organized tour. Major tour bus companies include:

Egged Tours
Tel: (03) 920 3992
www.eggedtours.com

United Tours
Tel: (03) 617 3333
www.unitedtours.co.il/english.asp

Tal Limousine VIP Services
Tel: (03) 975 4044
www.tal-limousine.com

H

HEALTH AND MEDICAL CARE

There are no vaccination requirements for tourists entering Israel except if they are arriving from infected areas. Israel has advanced health care services, with all citizens guaranteed medical attention by law. Visitors are advised to have medical insurance as even the shortest stay in hospital and elementary surgery is likely to cost thousands of dollars. Lists of doctors, dentists and duty pharmacies are available from hotel receptions or on the internet. Seeing a doctor is likely to cost at least $40. For more serious situations, go to a hospital emergency room (*checder miyun*). Sunburn, sunstroke and dehydration can be avoided by drinking large amounts of water and staying out of the sun. Tap water is as drinkable as anywhere in the developed world, with mineral water available everywhere.

L

LGBTQ TRAVELERS

Israel in general, and Tel Aviv in particular, are very tolerant of the LGBTQ community. Most cities, including Jerusalem, have an annual pride parade and LGBTQ clubs that fly the rainbow flag. Nevertheless, gay and lesbian, travelers would be advised to keep a lower profile in religious Jewish neighborhoods and Arab locations.

M

MONEY

Israel's currency is the New Israeli Shekel (NIS), and is divided into 100 agorot. Bills are issued in four denominations: 20 NIS (red); 50 NIS (green); 100 NIS (yellow); and 200 NIS (blue). Change comes in the bronze coins of 10 agorot and 50 agorot, and silver coins of 1 shekel, 2 shekels, 5 shekels and 10 shekels (silver and gold). Banks and bureaux de change are everywhere and it is usually more convenient in terms of time to change money at a bureau de change. The NIS is stable and floats freely against the world's major currencies, with a revised exchange rate each day.

P

POLICE

Due to the security situation, there is a strong police presence in Israel. There is also a conspicuous army presence, especially at checkpoints between Israel and the parts of the West Bank under Israeli control, and a tourist police presence at tourist hotspots Generally, police are amenable to helping those in distress. Police will hand out tickets to pedestrians crossing the road on a red light at traffic lights. Do not leave any packages unattended, as they are likely to be blown up by the anti-terrorist squad. For emergencies, call 100, and 110 for information.

POPULATION AND SIZE

With an annual growth rate of 2 percent, Israel's population reached 9 million in 2019. Its most populous cities are Jerusalem (pop. 900,000), Greater Tel Aviv (pop. 3.5 million), and Greater Haifa (pop. 700,000).

Area: 21,000 sq km (8,110 sq miles) including administered territories and Palestinian autonomous zones.

Highest mountain: Mount Hermon (2,766 meters/3,962ft).

Longest river: River Jordan (264km/165 miles).

POST OFFICE

Post offices branches can be identified by a logo of a white stag leaping across a red background. Post boxes are red. Letters take 5–9 days to reach Europe and America.

Major post offices are open all day, while smaller branches have variable opening hours. Post offices usually have a machine at the entrance dispending numbers, so that you do not have to wait in a line. Waiting time can be long but it is also possible to make an appointment online at www.israelpost.co.il, although this service is only available in Hebrew. On Friday afternoon, Saturday and public holidays post offices close all day. Other services at post offices include paying bills and traffic and parking fines, sending currency through Western Union, and currency exchange.

PUBLIC TRANSPORT

Visitors planning to spend much of their visit traveling on public transport are advised to purchase a Rav Kav Smart Card multi-travel ticket, which can be used interchangeably on buses, trains, the Jerusalem Light Rail, and Haifa Carmelit. The tickets can be purchased online at www.rail.co.il/en/pages/ravkavform.aspx or upon presentation of a valid passport at bus stations, railways stations, and other service points, including the railway station at Ben Gurion Airport. The cards provide considerable discounts including free intra-city extension trips after an inter-city trip, and multi-ride inter-city trips within a two-hour period. It also saves the inconvenience of searching for change when boarding buses and trains.

Buses are the most common means of public transport for both urban and inter-urban services. Egged and Dan (Greater Tel Aviv) were historically the dominant bus companies, but in recent years with routes subject to government tenders (to enhance competition), many smaller companies have gained ground including Superbus, Kavim, Nateev Express, and Metroplitine. Services are punctual and, if anything, impatient drivers tend to leave half a minute before time. If travelling to Eilat, it is advisable to reserve seats several days in advance. Buses do not run from Friday before sundown until Saturday after sundown. Inter-urban bus services start around 6am and finish in the early evening, except for the Tel Aviv–Jerusalem and Tel Aviv–Haifa lines, which continue until midnight. Urban services run from 5am to just after midnight.

The Jerusalem Central Bus Station is in Yafo, at the western entrance to the city. The Tel Aviv Central Bus Station is a vast shopping mall complex on Levinski in the south of the city (connected to Haganah train station) although there is also a large bus station in Arlozorov Street by Tel Aviv Savidor Central Station. Haifa has two bus stations: Hof Hacarmel (connected to the train station of the same name) at the city's southern entrance; and Checkpost, at the northern entrance to the city.

Trains. Israel Railways has undergone major expansion in recent years, and is good value, although tickets are more expensive than for comparable rides on buses. There is a station at Ben Gurion Airport, with a fast-link to Jerusalem and Tel Aviv and services to Haifa, Beer Sheva and all Israel's major cities except Eilat and the Upper Galilee (although there are new lines to Karmiel in the Western Galilee and Beit Shean in the Jordan Valley). Rather than taking the recently opened Jerusalem – Tel Aviv fast link (28 minutes), there are still services travelling on the scenic Ottoman route between Tel Aviv and Jerusalem via Beit Shemesh, the Judean Hills and the Jerusalem Biblical Zoo. There are no train services on the Sabbath, or on Jewish holidays. For more information, see www.rail.co.il.

Jerusalem Light Rail. A tram system operating from Pisgat Ze'ev in northern Jerusalem via the Old City's Damascus Gate, to the city center along Jaffa Road to the railway/central bus station, and on to Herzl Boulevard and Yad Vashem, in the southwest. Flat fare tickets can be purchased at www.citypass.co.il or at automatic ticket machines at each of the 22 stops on the line. Rav Kav cards can be used.

Tel Aviv Light Rail. This service, which will include and underground section in central Tel Aviv is still under construction. The first line – the Red Line – between Petah Tikva, Bnei Brak, Ramat Gan, Central Tel Aviv, and Jaffa, to Bat Yam – is in advanced stages of construction and is scheduled to open in 2021.

Carmelit/ Metro. Israel's only subway operates in Haifa and is called the Carmelit. This recently renovated system is in fact an underground cable car and is the quickest way of getting around Haifa. The train runs from Central Mount Carmel to downtown Haifa every 10 minutes, and makes six stops. The trip takes 9 minutes. It operates Sun–Thu 6am–10pm, Fri 6am to 1 hour before the Sabbath, and Sat from sunset to midnight. For more information, see http://www.carmelithaifa.com/.

Shared Taxis (*Sherut*). This is Israel's own indigenous mode of transport, operating in and between main cities every day, including on Shabbat. Individuals share a mini-bus or cab, which can take up to 10 people at a fixed price, usually equivalent to the bus fare for the same route. In Jerusalem *sheruts* between cities leave from near the central bus station and from near Kikar Tsiyon in the city center, including on Shabbat. In Tel Aviv the *sheruts* leave from near the Central Bus Station for Jerusalem, Haifa and most other cities. Local *sheruts*, especially in Tel

Aviv, follow the main bus routes, making similar stops in quicker time and charging the same fare. In all Israeli cities, taxi drivers will often follow bus routes charging a similar fare; but beware: they can become opportunistic about the price when faced with a tourist. For *sheruts* to and from the airport, see Airport.

Taxis offer a quick and convenient mode of travel in Israel. You can phone for a taxi in any major city, or hail one in the street. All urban taxis have meters, and their operation is compulsory. If the driver wants to turn off the meter he may be trying to take you for a ride in more ways than one: taxis are notorious for overcharging tourists. Tipping is not compulsory, but it is appreciated. Prices are fixed between cities, and the driver will tell you your fare in advance, or show you the official price list if you ask for it.

T

TELEPHONE

Israel's country code is 972 when phoning from abroad, and it is 970 for the Palestinian territories. There are few public phones remaining in Israel.

Area Codes in Israel

02 – Jerusalem
03 – Tel Aviv
04 – Northern Israel
08 – Southern Israel
09 – Herzliya and Netanya

Useful Numbers:

100 Police Emergency
110 Police Information
101 Ambulance
102 Fire Brigade
103 Electricity
166 Telephone repairs

199 Telephone company information

TIME ZONE

Israel is at Coordinated Universal Time UTC (GMT) +2: in other words 2 hours ahead of London in winter, and 1 hour in summer. Israel is 7 hours ahead of New York in winter, and 6 in summer.

TIPPING

If a service charge is not included for a meal at a restaurant, then 10–15 percent is expected. Israelis do not tip taxi drivers, but drivers will expect a small tip from tourists. Hotel staff such as porters (bell hops) should be tipped and hairdressers also expect a small tip.

TOURIST INFORMATION

There are helpful tourist information offices in London, New York as well all Israel's major cities. Visit the offical website of Israel's Ministry of Tourism (https://info.goisrael.com/en) for locations in Israel.

UK

London W1A 6GP

Tel: (20) 7299 1111

E-mail: sharone@goisrael.gov.il

US

New York

Tel: 1-212-499 5655

E-mail: info-ny@goisrael.gov.il

Chicago

Tel: 1-312-803 7080

E-Mail: JillD@goisrael.gov.il

Los Angeles

Tel: 1-323-658 7463

E-Mail: anatb@goisrael.com

VISAS AND PASSPORTS

For entry to Israel, tourists are required to hold passports that are valid for at least six months from the date of arrival. Stateless persons require a valid travel document with a return visa to the country of issue. Citizens of the US, Canada, the EU, Australia and New Zealand do not need a visa to enter Israel, only a valid passport. For citizens of these countries, there are no special health requirements.

Those entering Israel on holiday can stay for three months and are not allowed to work for money. Anyone wishing to enter the country for work, study or permanent settlement must apply for the appropriate visa at an Israeli Diplomatic or Consular Mission before leaving their own country.

All visitors to Israel, including diplomats, are required to fill in an entry form, AL-17, upon arrival. This form should be supplied on the flight to Israel. Visitors who intend visiting Muslim countries (except Egypt and Jordan) after their visit to Israel should ask the frontier control officer to put the entry stamp on this form instead of in their passports, as they may subsequently be refused entry into countries hostile towards Israel if an Israeli stamp appears on the passport.Tourists wishing to stay in Israel longer than three months must obtain an extension of stay.

WOMEN TRAVELERS

It is generally safe for women travelling alone. Local men may pester women but won't usually touch and will get the message if clearly given the cold shoulder. Women should dress modestly in religious areas and Jerusalem's Old City.

RECOMMENDED HOTELS

There is a wide choice of accommodations in Israel, although prices are relatively expensive ranging from hundreds of dollars per night in high-end hotels to $25 per night in a youth hostel. Unique Israeli forms of accommodations include kibbutz guesthouses (relatively expensive rural retreats) and Christian hospices (more luxurious than they sound, usually with a 19th-century European ambiance, and not to be confused with hospitals for the terminally ill). Both these offer an unusual taste of Israel. In the past decade, bed and breakfasts have become increasingly popular in Israel; while zimmerim are popular in northern Israel. Ideally this is some sort of country lodge, chalet or log cabin, in a rural retreat, though often it is a less romantic pre-fabricated structure. Youth hostels range from hole in the wall downtown joints through to the facilities of the Israel Youth Hostel Association, which are usually well appointed, and of three-star hotel quality (with prices to match). Then there is of course Airbnb, which can offer the best value as well as websites like Booking.com. Prices are usually far cheaper when booked as part of a package in advance.

$$$	over $200 per night
$$	$100-200 per night
$	Up to $100 per night

JERUSALEM

Addar $ *53 Nablus Road, tel: (02) 626 3111,* www.addar-hotel.com. A relatively new and comfortable, good-value Arab hotel with a warm, cosy atmosphere in a well-appointed building opposite St George's Cathedral. Near the Damascus Gate and Garden Tomb.

Arthur $$$ *13 Dorot Rishonim Street, tel: (02) 623 9999,* www.atlas.co.il/arthur-jerusalem Recently opened boutique hotel in the heart of downtown Jerusalem's pedestrian precinct, within easy walking distance of the Old City and Makhanei Yehuda market. Prides itself on its Israeli-style breakfasts, cosy atmosphere and retro-modern decor.

American Colony $$$ *1 Louis Vincent Street, off Nablus Road, tel: (02) 627 9777,* www.americancolony.com. Jerusalem's oldest hotel (not counting hospices) was established in 1881 by a Christian family. With its gourmet restaurants, landscaped gardens, stylish outdoor pool, and high-tech fitness room, the hotel has much character and charm and is favoured by the foreign press corps on account of its location between West and East Jerusalem.

Austrian Hospice $$ *37 Via Dolorosa, tel: (02) 626 5800,* www.austrian-hospice.com. Grand and ornate 19th-century building on the Via Dolorosa that served as a hospital for many years but was renovated in the late 1980s. An oasis of serenity amid the hubbub of the Old City and don't miss its authentic Viennese coffee house and central European cuisine with schnitzel, goulash and strudel.

Christmas $ *Ali Ibn Abi Taleb Street, tel: (02) 628 2588,* www.christmas-hotel.com. Attractive small boutique Arab hotel in the heart of East Jerusalem, with a delightful garden, attractive decor, comfortable rooms, and warm personal service.

Dan Jerusalem $$ *32 Lekhi, Mount Scopus, tel: (02) 533 1234,* www3.danhotels.com/JerusalemHotels/DanJerusalemHotel. With its stylish exteriors and interiors, outdoor patios and swimming pool, this large hotel sits atop Mount Scopus near the Hebrew University, far from the bustle of the city, and commands a breath-taking view of the Old City.

Holiday Inn Crowne Plaza $$ *Givat Ram, tel: (02) 658 8888,* www.ihg.com/crowneplaza/hotels/gb/en/jerusalem/. Landmark high-rise building at the Western entrance to the city, opposite the Central Bus Station and new railway station, offers luxury accommodation for modest prices and is convenient for touring locations outside of the city.

Inbal $$$ *3 Jabotinski, tel: (02) 675 6666,* www.inbalhotel.com. Overlooking the Liberty Bell Garden and Montefiore's windmill, this delightfully designed hotel with an attractive central inner courtyard, has attracted some world leaders away from the nearby King David.

King David Hotel $$$ *23 David ha-Melekh, tel: (02) 620 8888,* www3. danhotels.com/JerusalemHotels/KingDavidJerusalemHotel. Israel's premier hotel, where political leaders and the rich and famous often stay. It has style and an old-world ambiance, but in terms of quality of service its newer rivals try harder. Beautiful gardens and a swimming pool overlooking the Old City.

Little House in Baka $$ *1 Yehuda Street, off Hebron Road, tel: (02) 673 7944.* Cross between a boutique hotel and guesthouse in large, stylish 1920s home in Jerusalem's trendy Baka neighborhood.

Mamilla Hotel $$$ *11 Solomon Hamelekh Street, tel: (02) 548 2222,* www. mamillahotel.com. One of Jerusalem's newest hotels is also one of the city's most luxurious and inevitably most expensive. Best of all, the hotel is above the newly opened Mamilla shopping mall and adjacent to the Old City walls, with breath-taking views.

Mount Zion $$ *17 Hebron Road, tel: (02) 568 9555,* www.mountzion-jeru-salem.com. Originally an ophthalmology hospital built over a century ago, this building was converted into a stylish and ornate luxury hotel overlooking the Old City walls.

Notre Dame $$$ *3 Hatsanhanim Street, tel: (02) 627 9111,* https:// www.notredamecenter.org/. Luxurious accommodations, splendid 19th-century architecture and one of Jerusalem's best (non-kosher) restaurants. Superbly appointed hospice opposite the Old City walls and the New Gate. Vatican-owned, it has been extensively renovated and demonstrates that pilgrims in the 19th century knew how to enjoy life.

Our Sisters of Zion $$ *Ein Kerem, tel: (02) 641 5738,* http://www.notreda-medesion.org/centres/ein-kerem-guest-house/. Delightful pension in Ein Kerem. Spacious gardens filled with olive trees and grape vines. Comfortable rooms.

Palatin Hotel $ *4 Agrippas Street, tel: (02) 623 1141,* www.palatinhotel.com, *email:* info@palatinhotel.com, A clean and comfortable hotel, with a central location in West Jerusalem and close to the Makhane Yehuda market.

Prima Palace $$ *6 Pines Street, tel: (02) 531 1811,* www.prima-hotels-israel.com/PalaceHotel/Jerusalem. Colourful ultra-Orthodox establishment in the heart of West Jerusalem.

Ramat Rachel Hotel and Spa $$ *Kibbutz Ramat Rachel, tel: (02) 670 2555*. www.ramatrachel.co.il. Although within the city limits, the kibbutz grounds offer a stirring view of the Judean Desert. Comfortable accommodation and the kibbutz is adjacent to an unusual olive garden.

Scots Guesthouse $$ *St. Andrews Church 1 David Remez Street, tel: (02) 673 2401,* www.scotsguesthouse.com. Intimate Scots guesthouse atmosphere in central location by the old railway station. Haggis, mince pies, and mulled wine at Christmas; whisky all year round.

YMCA 3 Arches Hotel $$ *26 David Ha-Melekh tel: (02) 569 2652,* www.ymca3arches.com. Stylish 1930s building opposite the King David Hotel, designed by the same architect who planned the Empire State Building.

TEL AVIV

Cinema $$ *2 Zamenhoff, Dizengoff Circle, tel: (03) 520 7100,* www.cinemahotel.com. In the heart of Tel Aviv's café district this 80-room hotel is in a converted cinema and one of the city's finest examples of Bauhaus architecture.

City $ *9 Mapu Street, Tel Aviv, Tel: (03) 524 6253,* www.atlashotels.co.il. Near the beach and center of town, this clean and comfortable hotel puts an affordable roof over your head, in a good spot.

Crowne Plaza Hotel Tel Aviv City Center $$$ *132 Menachem Begin Road, tel: (03) 777 4000,* www.ihg.com/crowneplaza/hotels/us/en/tel-aviv/tlvcc/hoteldetail. On the upper floors of the iconic Azrieli Center. Offers splendid views of the city and is for businesspeople rather than beach lovers with only a view of the sea in the distance.

Dan Tel Aviv $$$ *99 Ha-Yarkon, tel: (03) 520 2525.* www.danhotels.com. The city's veteran luxury hotel offers excellent sea views and is renowned for comfort, style and convenience.

Fabric Hotel $$ *28 Nahlat Binyamin, tel: (03) 542 5555,* www.atlas.co.il/fabric-hotel/. The hotel, on the site of a former fabrics factory, contains a garden in a hidden courtyard and a hydroponic garden on its roof with a view of Tel Aviv's century-old original neighborhoods.

Lighthouse $$ 1 *Ben Yehuda Street, tel: (03) 766 0500,* www.brownhotels. com/lighthouse. Stylish boutique hotel in a rather unstylish high-rise building, one block from the beach.

Market House Hotel $$ *5 Beit Eshel Street, Jaffa, tel: (03) 797 4000,* https://www.atlas.co.il/market-house-hotel-tel-aviv-israel.   Stylish boutique hotel next to Jaffa's historic Clock Tower and renowned flea market, that takes its inspiration from the unique and authentic atmosphere of ancient Jaffa.

Montefiore $$$ *36 Montefiore Street, Tel Aviv, tel: (03) 564 6100.* Located in a 1920s building this really is a boutique hotel in the best sense of the word, with just 12 rooms. It is far from the sea, but if you can afford the hotel you can probably afford the taxi to the beach.

Norman $$$ *23-25 Nahmani Street, tel: (03) 543 5555.* World-class hotel in restored early 20th-century buildings, the Norman is a byword for class and style and the place where the wealthiest visitors to the city stay.

Tel Aviv Hilton $$$ *205 Hayarkon Street, tel: (03) 520 2222,* www3.hilton. com/en/hotels/israel/hilton-tel-aviv-TLVHITW/index.html. One of the city's most luxurious and fashionable hotels, with Tel Aviv high society, with prices to match. One minute from the beach thanks to its cliff-top location, and with a saltwater pool too.

GALILEE & GOLAN

Kibbutz Kfar Blum (Upper Galilee) $$ *Kfar Blum, Upper Galilee, tel: (04) 683 6611,* www.kfarblum-hotel.co.il. Comfortable accommodation in idyllic location along the banks of the River Jordan, in the Upper Galilee.

NAZARETH

Casa Nova Franciscan Hospice $ *Casa Nova Street, tel: (04) 645 6660.* Opposite the Basilica of the Annunciation. The Franciscan brothers lend the hospice an Italian atmosphere, which has the cuisine to go with it.

Fauzi Azar Inn $$$ *Near the Basilica of the Annunciation, tel: (04) 602 0469.* Converted Ottoman-style Arab mansion in the heart of old Nazareth. Very special accommodation.

Golden Crown $$ *2015 Street, Mount of the Precipice, tel: (04) 650 8000.* www.goldencrown.co.il. Large and very comfortable hotel on the edge of the city overlooking the Jezreel Valley.

SAFED

Ron $ *Hativat Yiftah Street, tel: (04) 697 2590.* Small, comfortable hotel in the heart of the old town.

Ruth Rimon Inn $$ *Artists' Quarter, Safed, tel: (04) 699 94666.* www.rimonim.com. Best hotel in the city, with relaxing hillside views and good rooms.

TIBERIAS

Aviv $ *66 Hagalil, tel: (04) 671 2272.* Conveniently located next to the old city of Tiberias.

Nof Ginosar Hotel $$ *Kibbutz Ginosar (near Tiberias), tel: (04) 670 0300,* www.ginosar.co.il. On the shores of the Sea of Galilee, close to the sacred Christian sites of Ein Tabgha and Capernaum.

Scots Hotel $$ *St. Andrews, tel: (04) 671 0710*. Converted from a 19th-century medical center, offers comfortable accommodation with rooms overlooking the Sea of Galilee.

HAIFA

Carmel Forest Spa $$$ *Carmel Forest, tel: (04) 830 7888*. www.isrotelexclusivecollection.com/carmel-forest. Located out of the city in the Carmel forest. Ideal for nature lovers, with a splendid view of the Mediterranean. Luxury accommodation and specialist spa treatments.

Carmelite Pilgrim Center $ *Stella Maris, POB 9047, Haifa 31090, tel: (04) 833 2084*. Carmelite sisters hospice on the slopes of Mount Carmel with good views of the bay.

Dan Carmel $$$ *85–87 Hanasi Boulevard, tel: (04) 830 6306*, www.danhotels.com. The city's most stylish hotel, located on Mount Carmel, with breath-taking view of Haifa Bay and the azure-colored Mediterranean.

Eden $ *8 Shmariyahu Levin Street, tel: (04) 866 4816*, http://www.eden-haifa.com/. Compact, convenient and comfortable in old stone building in the center of town.

DEAD SEA AND THE NEGEV

Ein Gedi Guest House $$ *Kibbutz Ein Gedi (Dead Sea), tel: (08) 659 4222*, http://en.ein-gedi.co.il/. Overlooking the remarkable Dead Sea and Judean Desert, unique spa with Dead Sea mud treatments, and a rare tropical garden. Ibexes and hyraxes roam the grounds.

Hod Hotel $ *Ein Bokek, Dead Sea, tel: (08) 668 8222*, www.hodhotel.co.il. Cheap and comfortable and near the Dead Sea in the main hotel district.

David Dead Sea Resort and Spa Hotel $$$ *Ein Bokek, tel: (08) 659 1234*, www.grandhotels-israel.com/david-dead-sea-hotel. This large hotel, formerly the Hyatt Regency, offers therapeutic treatment based on the Dead Sea's minerals and has a range of recreational facilities.

EILAT

Dan Eilat $$$ *North Beach, tel: (08) 636 2222*, www.danhotels.com. The flagship hotel of Israel's leading chain. Good service and good value.

Motel Aviv $ *126 Ofarim Street, tel. (08) 6371543*. Far from the beach, in the center of town but with a swimming pool.

Isrotel King Solomon's Palace $$ *North Beach, tel: (08) 636 3444*, www.isrotel.co.il. Elegantly designed hotel overlooking the marina with an excellent choice of restaurants. Consistently rated by guests as the city's best value hotel.

Prima Music $$ *Coral Beach, tel: (08) 638 8555*, www.prima-hotels-israel.com/. South of the main town near the more secluded Coral Beach, this music-themed hotel is very comfortable and offers a stirring view of the Red Sea and surrounding mountains.

Red Rock $ *1 Derekh Paamei Hashalom, tel: (08) 637 3171*. Great location by the beach and near the center of town, and good value. Comfortable but unexceptional.

DICTIONARY

ENGLISH – HEBREW

HEBREW ALPHABET

alef א	**vav** ו	**kaf** כ	**pe** פ
bet ב	**zayin** ז	**lamed** ל	**tzadi** צ
gimel ג	**khet** ח	**mem** מ	**kof** ק
dalet ד	**tet** ט	**nun** נ	**resh** ר
heh ה	**yod** י	**samekh** ס	**shin** ש
		ayin ע	**tav** ת

adj adjective   **adv** adverb   **BE** British English   **n** noun   **prep** preposition   **v** verb

A

able יכול / יכולה
  yakhol (m) / yekhola (f)
about לגבי *legabey*
above מעל *me-al*
accept v **(approval)** לקבל
  lekabel
access n גישה *gisha*
accessory אביזר *avizar*
accident תאונה *te-unah*
account חשבון
  kheshbon
ache כאב *ke-ev*
acupuncture טיפול בדיקור
  tipul Bedikur
adapter מתאם *mat-em*
address n כתובת *ktovet*
admission כניסה *knisah*
admitted אושפז *ushpaz*
after לאחר *le-akhar*
afternoon אחר הצהריים *akhar hatzohorayim*
again שוב *shuv*
against נגד *neged*
age גיל *gil*
air conditioning מיזוג אוויר *mizug avir*
air mattress מזרן אוויר *mizran avir*
airmail דואר אוויר *do-ar avir*
airplane מטוס *matos*
airport שדה תעופה *sdeh te-ufa*

aisle seat מושב ליד המעבר
  moshav leyad ha-ma-avar
alarm clock שעון מעורר *sha-on me-orer*
alcohol אלכוהול *alkohol*
alcoholic adj אלכוהולי *alkoholi*
allergic אלרגי / אלרגית *alergi (m) / alergit (f)*
allergic reaction תגובה אלרגית
  tguva alergit
alphabet אלף-בית *alef-bet*
also כמו כן *kmo khen*
alter v לשנות *leshanot*
altitude sickness מחלת גבהים *makhalat gvahim*
amazing מדהים *madhim*
amber ענבר *inbar*
ambulance אמבולנס
  ambulance
American אמריקאי / אמריקאית
  amerika-i (m) / amerika-it (f)
amethyst אחלמה *akhlama*
amount n **(money)** סכום *skhum*
amusement park פארק שעשועים
  park sha-ashu-im
analgesic משכך כאבים
  meshakekh ke-evim
and ו *ve*
anesthetic חומר מרדים *khomer mardim*
animal בעל חיים *ba-al kha-im*
ankle קרסול *karsol*
answer תשובה *tshuva*

antibiotic אנטיביוטיקה *antibyotika*

antidepressant נוגד דיכאון *noged dika-on*

antique עתיק *atik*

antiques store חנות עתיקות
khanut atikot

antiseptic cream
משחה לחיטוי *mishkha lekhitu*

any כלשהו / כלשהי *kolshehu* (m) / *kolshehi* (f)

anyone כל אחד / כלאחת *kol ekhad* (m) / *kol akhat* (f)

anything כל דבר שהוא *kol davarshehu*

anywhere כל מקום שהוא
kol makom shehu

apartment דירה *dirah*

aperitif אפריטיף *aperitif*

appendix תוספתן *tosaftan*

appliance מוצר חשמלי *mutzar khashmali*

appointment פגישה *pgisha*

arcade ארקדה *arkada*

architect ארכיטקט / ארכיטקטית *arkhitekt* (m) / *arkhitektit* (f)

arm זרוע *zro-a*

aromatherapy ארומתרפיה *aromaterapya*

around (approximately); (around the corner)
מעבר *me-ever*

arrival הגעה *haga-a*

arrive להגיע *lehagi-a*

art אמנות *amanut*

art gallery גלריית אמנות *galeryat amanot*

aspirin אספירין *aspirin*

assistance סיוע *siyu-a*

assorted מגוון *migvan*

asthma אסתמה *astma*

astringent
חומר עוצר דימום
khomer otzer dimum

at ב *be*

ATM כספומט *kaspomat*

attack n התקפה *hatkafa*

attend להשתתף *lehishtatef*

attractive מושך / מושכת *moshekh* (m) / *moshekhet* (f)

audio guide מדריך קולי
madrikh koli

Australia אוסטרליה *ostralya*

average ממוצע *memutza*

away הרחק *harkhek*

awful נורא *nora*

B

baby תינוק / תינוקת *tinok* (m) / *tinoket* (f)

baby bottle בקבוק לתינוק *bakbuk latinok*

baby food אוכל תינוקות *okhel tinokot*

baby wipes מגבונים לתינוק *magvonim latinok*

babysitter בייביסיטר *baybisiter*

back v לחזור *lakhazor*; n גב *gav*

backache כאב גב *ke-ev gav*

backpack תרמיל גב *tarmil gav*

bad רע / רעה *ra* (m) / *ra-a* (f)

bag (purse/ handbag); (shopping) תיק *tik*

baggage [BE] מטען *mitan*

baggage check בדיקת מטען
bdikat mitan

baggage claim קבלת מזוודות
kabalat mizvadot

bakery מאפיה *ma-afiya*

balance (finance) יתרה *yitra*

balcony מרפסת *mirpeset*

ballet בלט *balet*

bandage n תחבושת *takhboshet*

bank (finance) בנק *bank*

bank note שטר כסף *shtar kesef*

bar בר *bar*

barber ספר *sefer*

basket סל *sal*

basketball game משחק כדורסל *miskhak kadursal*

bath אמבטיה *ambatya*

bathing suit בגד ים *beged yam*

bathrobe חלוק רחצה *khaluk rakhatza*

bathroom שירותים *sherutim*

battery סוללה *solela*

battleground שדה קרב *sdeh krav*

be להיות *lihiyot*

beach ball כדור חוף
kadur khof

beard זקן *zakan*

beautiful יפה / יפה *yafe* (m) / *yafa* (f)

beauty salon מכון יופי *makhon yofi*

bed מיטה *mita*

before (time) לפני *lifney*

begin להתחיל *lehatkhil*
behind מאחור *me-akhor*
beige בז' *bezh*
bell (electric) פעמון *pa-amon*
below מתחת *mitakhat*
belt חגורה *khagora*
berth הניש שגרד *dargash she-na*
better יותר טוב *yoter tov*
between בין *beyn*
bicycle אופניים *ofana-im*
big גדול / גדולה *gadol (m) / gdola (f)*
bike route נתיב אופניים *netiv ofana-im*
bikini ביקיני *bikini*
bill (restaurant); (bank note) חשבון *kheshbon*
binoculars משקפת *mishkefet*
bird ציפור *tzipor*
birth לידה *leyda*
birthday יום הולדת *yom huledet*
black שחור *shakhor*
bladder שלפוחית *shalpukhit*
blade להב *lahav*
blanket שמיכה *smikha*
bleach מלבין *malbin*
bleed לדמם *ledamem*
blind (window) סירט *tris*
blister אבעבועה *ava-abuah*
blocked חסום / חסומה *khasum (m) / khasuma (f)*
blood דם *dam*
blood pressure לחץ דם *lakhatz dam*
blouse חולצה *khultza*
blow dry לעשות פן *la-asot fen*
blue כחול *kakhol*
boat סירה *sira*
boat trip יציאה להפלגה *yetziah lehaflaga*
body גוף *guf*
bone עצם *etzem*
book ספר *sefer*
booklet (of tickets) חוברת *khoveret*
bookstore חנות ספרים *khanut sfarim*
boot מגף *magaf*
boring משעמם *mesha-amem*
born נולד / נולדה *nolad (m) / nolda (f)*

botanical garden גן בוטני *gan botani*
botany בוטניקה *botanika*
bother לטרוח *litro-akh*
bottle בקבוק *bakbuk*
bottle opener פותחן בקבוקים *potkhan bakbukim*
bottom תחתית *takhtit*
bowel מעי *me-i*
bowl קערה *ke-ara*
box קופסה *kufsa*
boxing match תחרות אגרוף *takharut igruf*
boy ילד *yeled*
boyfriend חבר *khaver*
bra חזיה *khaziya*
bracelet צמיד *tzamid*
brake בלם *balam*
break (out of order) להתקלקל *hitkalkel*
breakdown (car) התקלקלה *hitkalkela*
breakfast ארוחת בוקר *arukhat Boker*
breast חזה *khazeh*
breathe לנשום *linshom*
bridge גשר *gesher*
bring להביא *lehavi*
bring down להוריד *lehorid*
British (person) בריטי / בריטית *briti (m) / britit (f)*
broken שבור / שבורה *shavur (m) / shvura (f)*
brooch סיכת נוי לבגד *sikat noy labeged*
broom מטאטא *matate*
brown חום *khum*
bruise חבורה *khavura*
brush n מברשת *mivreshet*
bucket דלי *dli*
bug חרק *kherek*
build לבנות *livnot*
building בניין *binyan*
burn לשרוף *lisrof*
bus אוטובוס *otobus*
bus station תחנת אוטובוס *takhanat otobus*
bus stop תחנת אוטובוס *takhanat otobus*
business card כרטיס ביקור *kartis bikur*
business center (at hotel) מרכז עסקים *merkaz asakim*
business class מחלקת עסקים *makhleket asakim*
business district מחוז עסקים *makhoz asakim*

business trip נסיעת עסקים *nesi-at asakim*
busy עסוק / עסוקה *asuk (m) / asuka (f)*
but אבל *aval*
butane gas גז בוטן *gaz butan*
butcher קצב *katzav*
button כפתור *kaftor*
buy לקנות *liknot*

C

cabin (ship) תא *ta*
cafe בית קפה *beyt kafe*
calculator מחשבון *makhshevon*
calendar לוח שנה *lu-akh shana*
call n (phone) שיחה; v; (summon) לקרוא *sikha likro*
calm רגוע / רגועה *ragu-a (m) / regu-a (f)*
camera מצלמה *matzlema*
camera case תיק למצלמה *tik lematzlema*
camera shop חנות למצלמות *khanut lematzlemot*
camp bed מיטת מחנה *mitat makhane*
camp מחנה להקים *lehakim makhane*
camping מחנאות *makhana-ut*
camping equipment ציוד למחנאות *tziud lemakhana-ut*
campsite אתר מחנאות *atar makhana-ut*
can opener פותחן *potkhan*
can v (be able to) יכול / יכולה *yakhol (m) / yekhola (f);*
n (container) פחית שימורים *pakhit shimurim*
Canada קנדה *kanada*
Canadian קנדי / קנדית *kanadi (m) / kanadit (f)*
cancel לבטל *levatel*
candle נר *ner*
candy store חנות ממתקים *khanut mamtakim*
cap מכסה *mikhse*
car מכונית *mekhonit*
car hire [BE] השכרת רכב *haskarat rekhev*
car mechanic מכונאי רכב *mekhona-i rekhev*
car park [BE] מגרש חניה *migrash khanaya*
car rental השכרת רכב *haskarat rekhev*
car seat מושב מכונית *moshav mekhonit*
carafe קנקן *kankan*
card (Greeting) כרטיס (ברכה) *kartis (brakha);*

(game) קלף *; klaf*
card game משחק קלפים *miskhak klafim*
cardigan קרדיגן *kardigan*
carry לשאת *laset*
cart עגלה *agala*
carton (of cigarettes) קרטון *karton*
case (camera) תיק *tik*
cash v לפדות; n כסף מזומן *lifdot ; kesef mezuman*
cashier קופאי / קופאית *kupa-i (m) / kupa-it (f)*
casino קזינו *kazino*
castle slot; סירה *tira*
caution זהירות *zehirut*
cave מערה *me-ara*
CD תקליטור *taklitor*
cell phone טלפון סלולרי *telefon selolari*
cemetery בית קברות *beyt kvarot*
center of town מרכז העיר *merkaz ha-ir*
centimeter סנטימטר *sentimeter*
ceramics קרמיקה *keramika*
certain בטוח / בטוחה *batu'akh (m) / betukha (f)*
certificate תעודה *te-uda*
chair כסא *kise*
change n עודף (money) ; v לפרוט *odef lifrot (money);* v (clothes, diaper) להחליף *lehakhlif*
charcoal פחם *pekham*
charge n; חיוב; v לחייב *khiyuv; lekhayev*
cheap זול *zol*
check (restaurant) n חשבון *kheshbon;* (banking) המחאה *hamka-ah;* v (someone, something) לבדוק *livdok*
check-in desk (airport) דלפק צ'ק-אין *dalpak chek-in*
checking account חשבון עובר ושב *kheshbon over vashav*
check out v לעשות צ'ק אאוט *la-asot chek awt*
check-up (medical) בדיקה *bdika*
cheers לחיים *lekha-im*
chef שף *shef*
chemical toilet בית שימוש כימי *beyt shimush khimi*
chemist [BE] כימאי / כימאית *khima-i (m) / khima-it (f)*

cheque [BE] המחאה
hmkha-ah

chess שחמט shakhmat

chess set שחמט ערכת erkat shakhmat

chest חזה khaze

chest pain בחזה כאבים ke-evim bakhaze

child ילדה / ילד yeled (m) / yalda (f)

child's seat לילד מושב
moshav layeled

children's clothing ילדים בגדי
bigdey yeladim

children's portion לילדים מנה
mana liyeladim

choice בחירה bkhira

church כנסיה knesiya

cigar סיגר sigar

cigarette סיגריה sigarya

cinema [BE] קולנוע kolnoa

classical קלאסי klasi

clean adj; נקיה / נקי naki (m)/nekiya(f) לנקות/ lenakot

cleansing cream ניקוי קרם krem nikuy

clear v לפנות lefanot

cliff צוק tzuk

clip לחתוך lakhtokh

clock שעון sha-on

close v לסגור lisgor

closed סגור sagur

cloth מטלית matlit

clothing ביגוד bigud

clothing store בגדים חנות
khanut bgadim

cloud ענן anan

coat n (clothing) מעיל me-il

coin מטבע matbe-a

cold (illness); הצטננות hitztanenut ; adj קר kar

collar צווארון tzavaron

colleague עמיתה / עמית
amit (m) / amita (f)

color צבע tzeva

comb מסרק masrek

come לבוא lavo

comedy קומדיה komedya

commission (fee) עמלה amla

common (frequent) נפוץ nafotz

compartment (train) תא ta

compass מצפן matzpen

complaint תלונה tluna

computer (PC) מחשב makhshev

concert הופעה hofa-a

concert hall קונצרטים אולם
ulam kontzertim

condom קונדום kondom

conference room ועידה חדר kheder ve-ida

confirm לאשר le-asher

confirmation אישור ishur

congratulations טוב מזל mazal tov

connect v לחבר lekhaber

connection (transportation, internet) חיבור
khibur

constipation עצירות atzirut

consulate קונסוליה konsulya

contact lens מגע עדשות
adashot maga

contagious מדבק medabek

contain v מכילה / מכיל mekhil (m)/mekhila (f)

contraceptive מניעה אמצעי
emtza-i meni-ah

contract חוזה khoze

control שליטה shlita

convention hall ועידות מרכז merkaz ve-idot

cooking facilities בישול מתקני mitkaney bishul

copper נחושת nekhoshet

corkscrew פקקים חולץ
kholetz pkakim

corner פינ pina

cost n עלות alut; v לעלות a-alot

cot מתקפלת מיטה mita mitkapelet

cotton כותנה kutna

cough n שיעול shi-ul

counter דלפק dalpak

country מדינה medina

countryside כפר kfar

court house המשפט בית beyt hamishpat

cover charge כניסה דמי
dmey knisah

cramps עוויות avit

crayon צבעון tzivon

cream (toiletry) קרם krem

credit אשראי ashray

credit card כרטיס אשראי *kartis ashray*
crib עריסה *arisa*
crockery [BE] כלי חרס *kli kheres*
cross-country skiing סקי למרחקים *ski lemerkhakim*
crossing (maritime) חצייה *khatzaya*
crossroads צמתים *tzmatim*
crown (Danish currency) קרונה *karona*
crystal בדולח *bdolakh*
cufflink חפת *khefet*
cuisine מטבח *mitbakh*
cup ספל *sefel*
currency מטבע *matbe-a*
currency exchange office משרד לחילופי מט"ח *misrad lekhilufey matakh*
current (ocean) זרם *zerem*
curtain וילון *vilon*
customs מכס *mekhes*
customs declaration form טופס הצהרת מכס *tofes hatzharat mekhes*
cut n (wound) חתך *khatakh*; **v (with scissors)** לגזור *ligzor*
cut glass זכוכית מלוטשת *zkhukhit meluteshet*
cycling race אופניים מרוץ *merotz ofanayim*

D

dairy חלב מוצרי *mutzarey khalav*
damaged פגום / פגומה *pagum (m) / pguma (f)*
dance club לילה מועדון *mo-adon layla*
dance n ריקוד *rikud*; **v** לרקוד *lirkod*
danger סכנה *sakana*
dangerous מסוכן *mesukan*
Danish (person); adj דני / דנית *deni (m) / denit (f)*
dark חשוך *khashukh*
date (appointment) פגישה *pgisha*; **(day)** תאריך *ta-arikh*
day יום *yom*
decision החלטה *hakhlata*
deck (ship) סיפון *sipun*
deck chair נוח כסא *kisse no-akh*
declare (customs) להצהיר *lehatzhir*

deep עמוק *amok*
degree (temperature) מעלה *ma-ala*
delay עיכוב *ikuv*
delicatessen מעדנייה *ma-adaniya*
delicious טעים *ta-im*
deliver להביא *lehavi*
delivery משלוח *mishlo-akh*
denim ג'ינס *jins*
Denmark דנמרק *denemark*
dentist שיניים רופא *rofe shinayim*
denture תותבת שן *shen totevet*
deodorant דיאודורנט *de-odorant*
depart לעזוב *la-azov*
department (shop) מחלקה *makhlaka*
department store כלבו חנות *khanut Kolbo*
departure עזיבה *aziva*
departure gate יציאה שער *sha-ar yetziah*
deposit n (bank); (down payment) הפקדה *hafkada*
dessert קינוח *kinu-akh*
detergent ניקוי חומר *khomer nikuy*
detour (traffic) מעקף *ma-akaf*
diabetic סוכרתי / סוכרתית *sukrati (m) / sukratit (f)*
diamond יהלום *yahalom*
diaper חיתול *khitul*
diarrhea שלשול *shilshul*
dictionary מילון *milon*
diesel דיזל *dizel*
diet דיאטה *dyeta*
difficult קשה / קשה *kashe (m) / kasha (f)*
digital דיגיטאלי / דיגיטאלית *digitali (m) / digitalit (f)*
dining car מסעדה קרון *karon misada*
dining room אוכל חדר *kheder okhel*
dinner ערב ארוחת *arukhat erev*
direct adj ; v (someone) לכוון ישיר *yashir lekhaven*
direction כיוון *kivun*
directory (phone) מדריך *madrikh*

dirty מלוכלך / מלוכלכת
melukhlakh (m) / melukhlekhet (f)

disabled נכה / נכה
nekhe (m) / nekkha (f)

disc (parking) תו (חניה)
tav (khanaya)

disconnect v (computer)
להתנתק lehitnatek

discount הנחה hanakha

disease מחלה makhala

dish (food item) מאכל ma-akhal

dishes (plates) כלים kelim

dishwasher מדיח כלים
medi-akh kelim

dishwashing detergent חומר ניקוי למדיח כלים
khomer nikuy lemedi-akh kelim

disinfectant חומר מחטא khomer mekhate

display case תיבת תצוגה teyvat tetzuga

district (of town) רובע rova

disturb להפריע lehafri-a

divorced גרוש / גרושה garush (m) / grusha (f)

dizzy סובל מסחרחורת / סובלת מסחרחורת
sovel miskharkhoret (m) /
sovelet miskharkhoret (f)

doctor רופא / רופאה rofe (m) / rofa (f)

doctor's office מרפאה mirpa-ah

dog כלב kelev

doll בובה buba

dollar (U.S.) דולר dolar

domestic (airport terminal) פנים ארצי pnim artzi

domestic flight טיסה פנים-ארצית tisa pnim artzit

double bed מיטה כפולה
mita kfula

double room חדר כפול kheder kaful

down למטה lemata

downtown area
אזור העיר התחתית ezor ha-ir hatakhtit

dozen תריסר treysar

dress n שמלה simla

drink n ; (cocktail); v משקה לשתות
mashke lishtot

drinking water מי שתיה mey shtiya

drip טפטוף tiftuf

drive לנהוג linhog

driver's license רשיון נהיגה rishyon nehiga

drop (liquid) טיפה tipa

drugstore בית מרקחת beyt merkakhat

dry יבש / יבשה yavesh (m) / yevesha (f)

dry cleaner ניקוי יבש nikuy yavesh

dummy [BE] (baby's) מוצץ motzetz

during במשך bemeshekh

duty (customs) מס mas

duty-free goods
מוצרים פטורים ממכס
mutzarim pturim mimekhes

duty-free shop חנות דיוטי-פרי khanut dyuti fri

dye צבע tzeva

E

each כל אחד kol ekhad

ear אוזן ozen

ear drops טיפות אוזניים tipot oznayim

earache כאב אוזניים ke-ev oznayim

early מוקדם mukdam

earring עגיל agil

east מזרח mizrakh

easy קל kal

eat לאכול le-ekhol

economy class מחלקת תיירים makhleket tayarim

elastic אלסטי elasti

electric חשמלי khashmali

electrical outlet שקע חשמלי sheka khashmali

electricity חשמל khashmal

electronic אלקטרוני elektroni

elevator מעלית ma-alit

e-mail האימייל haemail

e-mail address כתובת האימייל
ktovet haemail

embassy שגרירות shagrirut

embroidery ריקמה rikma

emerald אזמרגד izmargad

emergency חירום kherum

emergency exit יציאת חירום
yetziat kherum

empty ריק rek

enamel תזגיג tazgig

end לסיים lesayem

engaged (phone) תפוס tafus

England אנגליה anglia

English (language) אנגלית *anglit*; (person)
אנגלי/אנגליה *angli (m) / anglia (f)*
enjoyable מהנה *mehane*
enlarge להגדיל *lehagdil*
enough מספיק *maspik*
enter v enter somewhere ; enter IT content
להיכנס / להכניס
lehikanes; lehakhnis
entrance כניסה *knisa*
entrance fee דמי כניסה *dmey knisa*
entry (access) רשומה *reshuma*
envelope מעטפה *ma-atafa*
equipment ציוד *tziyud*
eraser מחק *makhak*
escalator מעלית *ma-alit*
estimate n ; (quotation) הצעת מחיר *hatza-at mekhir*
e-ticket כרטיס אלקטרוני *kartis elektroni*
e-ticket check-in
צ׳ק-אין עם כרטיס אלקטרוני
chek in im kartis elektroni
Europeה אירופ *eyropa*
European Union האיחוד האירופי
ha-ikhud ha-eyropi
evening ערב *erev*
every כל *kol*
everything הכל *hakol*
exchange rate שער החליפין *sha-ar hakhalifin*
exchange v (money) להמיר *lehamir*
excursion טיול *tiyul*
excuse v לתרץ *letaretz*
exhibition תערוכה *ta-arukha*
exit n ; v (computer) יציאה לצאת *yetziah latzet*
expect לצפות *litzpot*
expense הוצאה *hotza-a*
expensive יקר *yakar*
express לבטא *levate*
expression ביטוי *bituy*
extension (phone) שלוחה
shlukha
extra אקסטרה *extra*
eye עין *ayin*
eye drops טיפות עיניים *tipot eynayim*
eye shadow צללית לעין
tzlalit la-ayin

eyesight ראיה *re-iya*

F

fabric (cloth) בד *bad*
face פנים *panim*
facial טיפול פנים *tipul panim*
factory מפעל *mifal*
fair הוגן / הוגנת
hogen (m) / hogenet (f)
fall ליפול v *lipol*
family משפחה *mishpakha*
fan (device); (person)
מאוורר / הצי׳ריעם
*me-avrer (m); *
ma-aritz (m) / ma-aritza (f)
far רחוק / רחוקה *rakhok (m) / rekhoka (f)*
fare (ticket) דמי נסיעה *dmey nesi-a*
farm חווה *khava*
far-sighted רואי רחוק *rekhok ro-i*
fast adj מהיר / מהירה
mahir (m) / mehira (f)
fast-food place מסעדת מזון מהיר *misedet mazon mahir*
faucet ברז *berez*
fax פקס *fax*
fax number מספר פקס *mispar faks*
fee (commission) עמלה *amla*
feed v להאכיל *leha-akhil*
feel (physical state) להרגיש *lehargish*
ferry מעבורת *ma-aboret*
fever חום *khom*
few קומץ *kometz*
field שדה *sade*
file (for nails) פצירה *ptzira*
fill in (form) למלא *lemale*
filling (tooth) סתימה *stima*
film [BE] (v); (n) סרט ;להסריט *lehasrit; seret*
filter מסנן *mesanen*
find v למצוא *limtzo*
fine (OK) בסדר *beseder*
fine arts אמנויות יפות *omanuyot yafot*
finger אצבע *etzba*
fire אש *esh*
fire door דלת חסינת אש *delet khasinat esh*
fire escape יציאת חירום *yetziat kherum*
fire exit יציאת חירום *yetziat kherum*

first ראשון / ראשונה
rishon (m) / rishona (f)

first-aid kit ערכת עזרה ראשונה
erkat ezra rishona

first class מחלקה ראשונה
makhlaka rishona

first course מנה ראשונה mana rishona

fishing דייג dayig

fit v להתאים lehat-im

fitting room חדר מדידה kheder medida

fix v לתקן letaken

flashlight פנס panas

flat [BE] (apartment) דירה dira

flatware כלי אוכל kley okhel

flea market שוק הפשפשים
shuk hapishpeshim

flight טיסה tisa

floor רצפה ritzpa

florist חנות פרחים khanut prakhim

flower פרח perakh

flu שפעת shapa-at

fluid נוזל nozel

fog ערפל arafel

follow לעקוב la-akov

food אוכל okhel

food poisoning הרעלת מזון
haralat mazon

foot כף רגל kaf regel

football [BE] כדורגל kaduregel

for עבור avur

forbidden אסור asur

forecast תחזית takhazit

foreign זר zar

forest יער ya-ar

forget לשכוח lishko-akh

fork מזלג mazleg

form (document) טופס tofes

fountain (body of water) מעיין ma'ayan
(drinking facility) מעין birziya

frame (glasses) מסגרת misgeret

free בחינם bekhinam

freezer מקפיא makpi

fresh טרי tari

friend חבר / חברה
khaver (m) / khavera (f)

from מאת me-et

frost כפור kfor

frying pan מחבת לטיגון
makhvat letigun

full מלא male

full-time במשרה מלאה
bemisra belea

furniture ריהוט rihut

G

gallery גלריה galeria

game משחק miskhak

garage חניה מקורה khanaya mekura

garbage זבל zevel

garden גינה gina

gas דלק delek

gasoline דלק delek

gauze גאזה gaza

gem אבן חן even khen

general כללי klali

general delivery משלוח כללי
mishlo-akh klali

general practitioner [BE]
רופא משפחה
rofe mishpakha

genuine מקורי mekori

get (find) להשיג lehasig

get off לרדת laredet

get up לעלות la-alot

gift מתנה matana

gift shop חנות מתנות khanut matanot

girl ילדה yalda

girlfriend חברה khavera

give לתת latet

gland בלוטה baluta

glass (drinking) כוס kos

glasses (optical) משקפיים mishkafa-im

glove כפפה kfafa

glue דבק devek

go away לעזוב la-azov

go back לחזור lakhazor

go out לצאת latzet

gold זהב zahav

golf club מועדון גולף mo-adon golf

golf course מגרש גולף migrash golf

golf tournament טורניר גולף turnir golf

good טוב / טובה tov (m) / tova (f)

good afternoon אחר צהריים טובים akhar tzohora-im Tovim

good evening ערב טוב erev tov

good morning בוקר טוב boker tov

good night לילה טוב layla tov

goodbye להתראות lehitra-ot

gram גרם gram

grandchild נכד nekhed

gray אפור afor

great (excellent) נהדר nehedar

Great Britain בריטניה britanya

green ירוק yarok

greengrocer's [BE] ירקן yarkan

greeting ברכה brakha

ground-floor room [BE] חדר בקומת קרקע kheder bekomat karka

groundsheet יריעת קרקע yeri-at karka

group קבוצה kvutza

guesthouse בית הארחה beyt ha-arakha

guide dog כלב נחיה kelev nekhiya

guide מדריך / מדריכה madrikh (m) / madrikha (f)

guidebook מדריך טיולים madrikh tiyulim

gym חדר כושר kheder kosher

gynecologist רופא נשים / רופאת נשים rofe nashim (m) / rofat nashim (f)

H

hair שיער se-ar

hair dryer מייבש שיער meyabesh Se-ar

hairbrush מברשת לשיער mivreshet Lase-ar

haircut תספורת tisporet

hairdresser ספר / ספרית sapar (m) / saparit (f)

hairspray ספריי לשיער sprey lase-ar

hall (room) אולם ulam

hammer פטיש patish

hammock ערסל arsal

hand יד yad

hand cream קרם לידיים krem Layadayim

hand washable לרחיצה ביד lirkhitza Bayad

handbag [BE] תיק tik

handicrafts מלאכת יד melekhet yad

handkerchief מטפחת mitpakhat

handmade תוצרת יד totzeret yad

hanger קולב kolav

happy שמחה / שמח same-akh (m) / smekha (f)

harbor נמל namal

hard קשה kashe

hardware store חנות לחומרי בנייין khanut lekhomrey binyan

hare ארנבת arnevet

hat כובע kova

have (must) חייב khayav;

have (possess) יש yesh

hay fever קדחת השחת kadakhat hashakhat

head ראש rosh

headache כאב ראש ke-ev rosh

headlight פנס קדמי panas kidmi

headphones אוזניות ozniyot

health food store חנות טבע khanut teva

health insurance ביטוח בריאות bitu-akhbri-ut

hearing-impaired לקוי שמיעה / לקויית שמיעה lekuy shmi-a (m) / lekuyat Shmi-a (f)

heart לב lev

heart attack התקף לב hetkef lev

heat v לחמם lekhamem

heating חימום khimum

heavy כבד / כבדה kaved (m) / kveda (f)

hello שלום shalom

helmet קסדה kasda

help; (oneself) לעזור la-azor

here כאן kan

hi שלום shalom

high adj גבוה / גבוהה gavoha

gavo-a (m) / gvoha (f)

high tide גאות ge-ut

highchair כיסא האכלה kise ha'akhala

highway כביש מהיר kvish mahir

hill גבעה giv-a

hire [BE] v להעסיק leha-asik

history היסטוריה historya

hole חור khor

holiday; [BE] (vacation) חופשה khufsha

home בית bayit

horseback riding
רכיבה על סוסים rekhiva al susim

hospital בית חולים beyt kholim

hot (temperature) חם kham

hotel בית מלון beyt malon

hotel directory מדריך מלונות madrikh melonot

hotel reservation הזמנה למלון hazmana lemalon

hour (time) שעה sha'a

house בית bayit

how איך eykh

how far כמה רחוק kama rakhok

how long עוד כמה זמן
od kama zman

how many כמה kama

how much כמה kama

hug v לחבק lekhabek

hungry רעב / רעבה
ra-ev (m) / re-eva (f)

hunting צייד tzayad

hurry למהר lemaher

hurt (v) לפגוע lifgo-a; (adj) פצוע פצועה patzu-a
(m) / ptzu-a (f)

husband בעל ba-al

I

I אני ani

ice קרח eerakh

icy (weather) קפוא kafu

identification (card) מסמך זיהוי mismakh zihuy

if אם im

ill [BE] חולה / חולה
khole (m) / khola (f)

illness מחלה makhala

important חשוב khashuv

imported מיובא meyuba

impressive מרשים / מרשימה
marshim (m) / marshima (f)

in בתוך betokh

include כולל kolel

indoor מקורה mekure

inexpensive לא יקר lo yakar

infected מזוהם mezoham

infection זיהום zihum

inflammation דלקת daleket

information מידע meyda

information desk דוכן מודיעין dukhan modi'in

injection זריקה zrika

injure לפצוע liftzoa

injury פציעה ptzi-a

inn פונדק pundak

innocent חף מפשע khaf mipesha (m)
/ khafa mipesha (f)

inquiry שאלה sh'ela

insect bite עקיצה akitza

insect repellent דוחה חרקים
dokheh kharakim

insect spray תרסיס נגד חרקים
tarsis neged kharakim

inside בתוך betokh

instant messenger
שירות הודעות מיידיות
sherut hoda-ot miyadiyot

insurance ביטוח bitu-ach

insurance claim תביעת ביטוח
tvi-at bitu-ach

interest (finance) ריבית ribit

interested מעוניין / מעוניינת
me-unyan (m) / me-unyenet (f)

interesting מעניין / מעניינת
me-anyen (m) / me-anyenet (f)

international ; (airport terminal) בינלאומי beynle-umi

international flight
טיסה בינלאומית tisa beynle-umit

internet אינטרנט internet

internet cafe בית קפה אינטרנט
beyt kafe internet

interpreter מתורגמן / מתורגמנית
meturgeman (m) / meturgemanit (f)

intersection צומת tzomet

introduce להכיר *lehakir*
introduction (social) היכרות *heykerut*
investment השקעה *hashka'a*
invitation הזמנה *hazmana*
invite v להזמין *lehazmin*
invoice חשבונית *kheshbonit*
iodine יוד *yod*
Ireland אירלנד *irland*
Irish (person) אירי / אירית *iri (m) / irit (f)* ;
  adj מאירלנד *me-irland*
iron n (clothing); v מגהץ לגהץ *maghetz legahetz*
itemized bill חשבון מפורט *kheshbon meforat*

J

jacket ז'קט *zhaket*
jar (container) צנצנת *tzintzenet*
jaw לסת *leset*
jazz ג'ז *jez*
jeans ג'ינס *jins*
jet ski אופנוע ים *ofanoa yam*
jeweler תכשיטן/תכשיטנית *takhshitan (m) / takhshitanit (f)*
join v להצטרף *lehitztaref*
joint (anatomy) מפרק *mifrak*
journey מסע *masa*
just (only) רק *rak*

K

keep להחזיק *lehakhzik*
kerosene קרוסין *kerosin*
key מפתח *mafte-akh*
key card כרטיס מפתח *kartis mafte-akh*
kiddie pool בריכה לילדים *breykha liyladim*
kidney כליה *kilya*
kilogram קילוגרם *kilogram*
kilometer קילומטר *kilometer*
kind adj; סוג לב סוב *tuv lev sug*
kiss v לנשק *lenashek*
knee ברך *berekh*
knife סכין *sakin*

knitwear סריג *sarig*
knock לדפוק *lidfok*
know לדעת *lada-at*

L

label תווית *tavit*
lace תחרה *takhara*
lactose intolerant בלח ירצומל שיגר /
  בלח ירצומל השיגר *ragish lemutzarey khalav (m) / regisha lemutzarey khalav (f)*
lake אגם *agam*
lamp מנורה *menora*
landscape נוף *nof*
language שפה *safa*
lantern פנס *panas*
large גדול / גדולה *gadol (male) / gdola (female)*
last (adj) אחרון/אחרונה
  (v) להישאר *lehisha-er akharon (m) / akhrona (f)*
late (time) ; (delay) מאוחר איחור *meukhar ikhur*
laugh צחוק *tzkhok*
launderette [BE] מכבסה *makhbesa*
laundromat מכבסה אוטומטית *makhbesa Otomatit*
laundry כביסה *kvisa*
laundry facilities מתקני כביסה *mitkaney kvisa*
laundry service שירות כביסה *sherut kvisa*
lawyer עורך דין / עורכת דין *orekh din (m) / orekhet din (f)*
laxative חומר משלשל *khomer meshalshel*
leather עור *or*
leave v; (behind) לעזוב *la-azov*
left שמאל *smol*
left-luggage office [BE] שירות שמירת חפצים *sherut shmirat khafatzim*
leg רגל *regel*
lens (camera) ; (glasses) עדשה *adasha*
less פחות *pakhot*
lesson שיעור *she-ur*
letter מכתב *mikhtav*
library ספריה *sifriya*
license (driving) רישיון *rishayon*
life boat סירת הצלה *sirat hatzala*
life guard (beach) מציל *matzil*

life jacket חגורת הצלה
khagorat hatzala

life preserver חגורת הצלה
khagorat hatzala

lift [BE] **elevator** מעלית *ma-alit*

light (color) בהיר *bahir*;
(weight) קל *kal*

light bulb נורה *nura*

lighter מצית *matzit*

lightning ברק *barak*

like; (please) הצור *rotze (m) / rotza (f)*

linen מצעים *matza-im*

lip שפה *safa*

lipstick שפתון *sfaton*

liquor store חנות משקאות חריפים *khanut mashka-ot kharifim*

listen להקשיב *lehakshiv*

liter ליטר *liter*

little (amount) קצת *ktzat*

live *v* לחיות *likhyot*

loafers מוקסינים *mokasinim*

local מקומי *mekomi*

log off להתנתק *lehitnatek*

log on להתחבר *lehitkhaber*

login כניסה למערכת *knisa lama-arekhet*

long ארוך *arokh*

long-sighted [BE]
רחוק-ראיה / רחוקת ראיה
rekhok re-iya (m) / rekhokat re-iya (f)

look *v* להסתכל *lehistakel*

lose לאבד *le-abed*

loss אובדן *ovdan*

lost אבוד *avud*

lost and found מחלקת אבידות *makhleket avedot*

lost property office [BE]
מחלקת אבידות *makhleket avedot*

lotion תחליב *takhliv*

loud (voice) קולני *kolani*

love *v* לאהוב *le-ehov*

lovely מקסים *maksim*

low נמוך / נמוכה *namukh (m) / nemukha (f)*

low tide שפל *shefel*

luck מזל *mazal*

luggage מטען *mitan*

luggage cart עגלת מזוודות *eglat mizvadot*

luggage locker תא אחסון
ta ikhsun

lunch ארוחת צהריים *arukhat tzohora-im*

lung ריאה *re-a*

M

magazine כתב עת *ktav et*

magnificent מקסים *maksim*

maid *n* עוזרת בית *ozeret Ba-it*

mail *n* דואר *do-ar*; *v*
לשלוח בדואר *lishlo-akh bado-ar*

mailbox תבת דואר *tevat do-ar*

make-up רופיא *lpur*

mall קניון *kenyon*

mallet פטיש עץ *patish etz*

man גבר *gever*

manager מנהל / מנהלת
menahel (m) / menahelet (f)

manicure מניקור *manikur*

many רבים *rabim*

map מפה *mapa*

market *n* שוק *shuk*

married נשוי / נשואה
nasuy (m) / nesu-a (f)

mass (religious service) מיסה *misa*

massage עיסוי *isuy*

match *n* **(sport)** תחרות
takharut

material חומר *khomer*

matinée הצגה יומית *hatzaga yomit*

mattress מזרן *mizran*

may *v* אולי *ulay*

meadow אחו *akhu*

meal ארוחה *arukha*

mean *v* להתכוון *lehitkaven*

measure למדוד *limdod*

measuring cup כוס מדידה
kos medida

measuring spoon כף מדידה
kaf medida

mechanic מכונאי *mekhona-i*

medicine (drug) תרופה *trufa*

meet לפגוש *lifgosh*

memorial אזכרה *azkara*

memory card כרטיס זיכרון *kartis zikaron*

mend לתקן *letaken*
menu תפריט *tafrit*
message הודעה *hoda-a*
meter מטר *meter*
middle אמצע *emtza*
midnight חצות *khatzot*
mileage מרחק במיילים *merkhak bemaylim*
minute דקה *daka*
mirror מראה *mara*
miscellaneous שונות *shonot*
Miss עלמה *alma*
miss v (lacking) לפספס *lefasfes*
mistake טעות *ta-ut*
mobile phone [BE] טלפון סלולרי *telefon selolari*
moisturizing cream קרם לחות *krem lakhut*
moment רגע *rega*
money כסף *kesef*
money order המחאת דואר *hamkha-at do-ar*
month חודש *khodesh*
monument מצבת זיכרון *matzevat zikaron*
moon ירח *yare-akh*
mop n מגב *magav*
moped סוסטוס *tustus*
more עוד *od*
morning בוקר *boker*
mosque מסגד *misgad*
mosquito net רשת נגד יתושים *reshet neged yatushim*
motel מוטל *motel*
motorboat סירת מנוע *sirat manoa*
motorcycle אופנוע *ofano-a*
motorway [BE] כביש מהיר *kvish mahir*
moustache שפם *safam*
mouth פה *pe*
mouthwash מי פה *mey pe*
move v לזוז *lazuz*
movie סרט *seret*
Mr. מר *mar*
Mrs. גברת *geveret*
much הרבה *harbeh*
mug n ספל *sefel*

mugging לשדוד *lishdod*
muscle שריר *shrir*
museum מוזיאון *muze-on*
music מוסיקה *musika*
musical מחזמר *makhazemer*
must (have to) חייב / חייבת *khayav (m) / khayevet (f)*

N

nail (body) ציפורן *tziporen*
nail clippers קוצץ ציפורניים *kotzetz tziporna-im*
nail file פצירת ציפורניים *ptzirat tziporna-im*
nail salon סלון יופי *salon yofi*
name שם *shem*
napkin מפית *mapit*
nappy [BE] חיתול *khitul*
narrow צר *tzar*
nationality לאום *le-om*
natural טבעי *tivi*
nausea בחילה *bkhila*
near קרוב *karov*
nearby ליד *leyad*
near-sighted קצר ראיה / קצרת ראיה *ktzar re-iya (m) / kitzrat re-iya (f)*
neck צוואר *tzavar*
necklace מחרוזת *makhrozet*
need v להזדקק *lehizdakek*
needle מחט *makhat*
nerve עצב *etzev*
never לעולם לא *le-olam Lo*
new חדש *khadash*
newspaper עיתון *iton*
newsstand דוכן עיתונים *dukhan itonim*
next אבא *haba*
next to ליד *leyad*
nice (beautiful) נחמד *nekhmad*
night לילה *layla*
no לא *lo*
noisy רועש *ro-esh*
none אף אחד *af ekhad*
non-smoking לא מעשנים *lo me-ashnim*
noon צהריים *tzohora-im*
normal נורמלי *normali*

north צפון *tzafon*
nose אף *af*
not לא *lo*
note (bank note) שטר *shtar*
notebook מחברת *makhberet*
nothing כלום *klum*
notice (sign) הודעה *hoda-a*
notify להודיע *lehodi-a*
novice מתחיל / מתחילה
matkhil (m) / matkhila (f)
now עכשיו *akhshav*
number מספר *mispar*
nurse אחות *akhot*

O

o'clock השעה *hasha-a*
occupation מקצוע *miktzo-a*
occupied תפוס *tafus*
office משרד *misrad*
off-licence [BE] מחוץ לרישיון
mikhutz larishayon
oil שמן *shemen*
old ישן *yashan*
old town העיר העתיקה *ha-ir ha-atika*
on על *al*
on time בזמן *bazman*
once פעם אחת *pa-am akhat*
one-way ticket כרטיס הלוך
kartis halokh
only רק *rak*
open *adj* פתוח *patu-akh*; *v* לפתוח
lifto-akh
opera אופרה *opera*
operation תפעול *tif-ul*
operator מפעיל *mafil*
opposite ההפך *hahefekh*
optician אופטיקאי *optika-i*
or או *o*
orange (color) כתום *katom*
orchestra תזמורת *tizmoret*
order *n* לצוות *tzav* **[decree]**; *v* צו; סדר; *seder*
[tidy]; *letzavot*
out of order מקולקל *mekulkal*
out of stock אזל מהמלאי
azal mehamelay

outlet (electric) שקע חשמלי
sheka khashmali
outside בחוץ *bakhutz*
oval סגלגל *sgalgal*
overlook *n* תצפית *taztzpit*
oxygen treatment טיפול עם חמצן *åtipul im*
khamtzan

P

pacifier (baby's) מוצץ
motzetz
packet חפיסה *hhafisa*
pad (sanitary) תחבושת
takhboshet
pail דלי *dli*
pain כאב *ke-ev*
painkiller משכך כאבים
meshakech Ke-evim
paint *n*; *v* צבע לצבוע
tzeva litzboa
painting צביעה *tzvi-a*
pair זוג *zug*
pajamas פיג׳מה *pijama*
palace ארמון *armon*
palpitations פלפיטציה
palpitatzia
pants מכנסיים *mikhnasayim*
panty hose גרבונים *garbonim*
paper נייר *neyar*
paper towel מגבת נייר *magevet neyar*
parcel [BE] חבילה *khavila*
parents הורים *horim*
park *n* פארק; *park*; *v* לחנות *lakhanot*
parking חניה *khanaya*
parking disc תו חניה *tav khanaya*
parking garage חניה מקורה
khanaya mekora
parking lot מגרש חניה
migrash khanaya
parking meter מדחן *madkhan*
part חלק *khelek*
part-time חלקי *khelki*
party (social gathering) מסיבה *mesiba*
passport דרכון *darkon*
passport control ביקורת דרכונים *bikoret darkonim*

passport photo תמונת פספורט *tmunat pasport*
paste (glue) להדביק *lehadbik*
pastry shop קונדיטוריה *konditurya*
patch טלאי *tlay*
path דרך *derekh*
patient מטופל / מטופלת
  metupal (m) / metupelet (f)
pattern דפוס *dfus*
pay לשלם *leshalem*
payment תשלום *tashlum*
peak n **(mountain)** פסגה *pisga*
pearl פנינה *pnina*
pedestrian הולך רגל *holekh regel*
pediatrician
  רופא ילדים / רופאת ילדים
  rofe yeladim (m) / rofat yeladim (f)
pedicure פדיקור *pedikur*
peg (tent) יתד *yated*
pen עט *rt*
pencil עיפרון *iparon*
pendant תליון *talyon*
penicillin פניצילין *penitzilin*
per day ליום *leyom*
per hour לשע *lesha-ah*
per person לאדם *le-adam*
per week לשבוע *leshavu-ah*
percentage אחוז *akhuz*
perfume בושם *bosem*
perhaps אולי *ulay*
period (monthly) מחזור *makhzor*
permit n **(fishing)**
  ; (hunting) היתר *heyter*
person אדם *adam*
personal אישי *ishi*
petite קטנה *ktana*
petrol [BE] דלק *delek*
pewter פיוטר *pyuter*
pharmacy בית מרקחת
  beyt mirkakhat
phone card כרטיס חיוג *kartis khiyug*
photo תמונה *tmuna*
photocopy צילום *tzilum*
photograph תמונה *tmuna*
photography צילום *tzilum*
phrase ביטוי *bituy*

pick up v **(go get)** לקבל *lekabel*
picnic פיקניק *piknik*
picnic basket סלסלת פיקניק
  salsalat piknik
piece חתיכה *khatikha*
pill גלולה *glula*
pillow כרית *karit*
PIN קוד סודי *kod sodi*
pin n **(brooch)** סיכה *sika*
pink ורוד *varod*
pipe מקטרת *mikteret*
place מקום *makom*
plane fly מטוס *matos*
planetarium מצפה כוכבים
  mitzpe kokhavim
plaster [BE] (bandage) פלסטר *plaster*
plastic פלסטיק *plastik*
plastic bag שקית ניילון
  dakit naylon
plastic wrap ניילון נצמד
  naylon nitzmad
plate צלחת *tzalakhat*
platform [BE] (station) רציף *ratzif*
platinum פלטינה *platina*
play n הצגה *hatzaga* **(theatre)**
  ; v לשחק *lesakhek*
playground מגרש משחקים
  migrash miskhakim
playpen לול *lul*
please בבקשה *bevakasha*
plug (electric) תקע חשמלי
  teka Khashmali
plunger פומפה *pompa*
pneumonia דלקת ריאות *daleket re-ot*
pocket כיס *kis*
point of interest נקודת עניין
  nekudat inyan
point v להצביע *lehatzbi-a*
poison רעל *ra-al*
poisoning הרעלה *harala*
pole (ski); (tent) מוט *mot*
police משטרה *mishtara*
police report דו"ח משטרתי *dokh mishtarti*
police station תחנת משטרה
  takhanat mishtara

pond אגם *agam*
pool בריכה *brekha*
porcelain חרסינה *kharsina*
port נמל *namal*
portable נישא *nisa*
porter סבל *sabal*
portion חלק *khelek*
post [BE] n דואר *do-ar*; v לשלוח בדואר *lishlo-akh bado-ar*
post office משרד הדואר *misrad hado-ar*
postage דמי ביול *dmey biyul*
postage stamp בול דואר *bul do-ar*
postcard גלויה *gluya*
pot סיר *sir*
pottery כלי חרס *kli kheres*
pound (British currency, weight) פאונד *pa-und*
powder אבקה *avka*
pregnant בהריון *beherayon*
premium (gas/ petrol) פרימיום *primyum*
prescribe לתת במרשם *latet bemirsham*
prescription מרשם *mirsham*
present n מתנה *matana*
press (iron) גיהוץ בקיטור *gihutz bekitor*
pressure לחץ *lakhatz*
pretty יפה / יפה *yafe (m) / yafa (f)*
price מחיר *mekhir*
price-fixed menu תפריט במחיר קבוע *tafrit bemekhir kavu-a*
print n **(photo)** תדפיס *tadpis*; v **(document)** להדפיס *lehadpis*
private פרטי *prati*
profit n רווח *revakh*
program (of events) תוכנית *tokhnit*
pronounce v להגות *lahagot*
pronunciation n הגיה *hagiya*
provide לספק *lesapek*
pull v למשוך *limshokh*
pump משאבה *masheva*
puncture פנצ'ר *pancher*
purchase n קניה *kniya*; v לקנות *liknot*

pure טהור *tahor*
purple סגול *sagol*
purse (handbag) תיק יד *tik Yad*
push v דחוף *lidkhof*
pushchair [BE] עגלת ילדים *eglat Yeladim*
put לשים *lasim*

Q

quality איכות *eykhut*
quantity כמות *kamut*
question n שאלה *she-ela*
quick מהר *maher*
quiet שקט *shaket*

R

race מירוץ *meyrotz*
race track מסלול המירוצים *maslul hameyrotzim*
racket (sport) מחבט *makhbet*
radio רדיו *radyo*
railway station [BE] תחנת רכבת *takhanat rakevet*
rain גשם *geshem*
raincoat מעיל גשם *me-il geshem*
rape n אונס *ones*
rash פריחה *prikha*
rate n **(exchange)** ; **(price)** תעריף *ta-arif*
razor סכין גילוח *sakin gilu-akh*
razor blade סכין גילוח *sakin gilu-akh*
ready מוכן / מוכנה *mukhan (m) / mukhana (f)*
real (genuine) אמיתי *amiti*
rear מאחור *me-akhor*
receipt קבלה *kabala*
reception קבלה *kabala*
receptionist פקידת קבלה *pkidat kabala*
recommend להמליץ *lehamlitz*
rectangular מלבני *malbeni*
red אדום *adom*
reduction הפחתה *hafkhata*
refrigerator מקרר *mekarer*
refund v להחזיר *lehakhzir*
regards n הערכה *ha-arakha*; להתייחס *lehityakhes*
region איזור *ezor*
registered mail דואר רשום *do-ar rashum*

registration הרשמה *harshama*
regular (gas / petrol) רגיל *ragil*
relationship מערכת יחסים *ma-arekhet yakhasim*
reliable אמין *amin*
religion דת *dat*
rent v לשכור *liskor*
rental השכרה *haskara*
rental car מכונית שכורה *mekhonit skhura*
repair תיקון *tikun*; v לתקן *letaken*
repeat לחזור *lakhazor*
report (theft) לדווח *ledaveakh*
request n בקשה *bakasha*; v לבקש *levakesh*
required דרוש *darush*
requirement דרישה *drisha*
reservation הזמנה *hazmana*
reservations office משרד הזמנות *misrad hazmanot*
reserve לשמור *lishmor*
reserved שמור *shmor*
rest n מנוחה *menukha*
restaurant מסעדה *misada*
restroom שירותים *sherutim*
retired adj גמלאי / גמלאית *gimla-I (m)/gimla-it (f)*; v לצאת לגמלאות *latzet legimla-ot*
return (come back); (give back) לחזור; להחזיר *lakhazor; lehakhzir*
return ticket [BE] כרטיס הלוך\כרטיס הלוך חזור *kartis halokh/kartis halokh khazur*
rib צלע *tzela*
ribbon סרט *seret*
right (correct) נכון *nakhon*; (direction) ימין *yamin*
ring (jewelry) טבעת *taba-at*
   ring (bell) לצלצל *letzaltzel*
river נהר *nahar*
road דרך *derekh*
road assistance שירותי דרך *sherutey Derekh*
road map מפת דרכים *mapat drakhim*
road sign תמרור *tamrur*
robbery שוד *shod*
romantic רומנטי *romanti*
room (hotel); (space) חדר ; מקום *kheder; makom*
room number מספר חדר *mispar kheder*
room service שירות חדרים

room service שירות חדרים
   sherut khadarim
room temperature
   טמפרטורה בחדר *temperatura bakheder*
rope חבל *khevel*
round עגול *agol*
round (golf) סבב *sevev*
round-trip ticket
   כרטיס הלוך ושוב
   kartis halokh vashov
route נתיב *nativ*
rowboat סירת משוטים *sirat meshotim*
rubber (material) גומי *gumi*
rubbish [BE] זבל *zevel*
ruby אודם *odem*

S

Sabbath שבּת *shabbat*
safe n (vault) כספת *kasefet*; (not in danger) בטוח / בטוחה
   batu-akh (m) / betukha (f)
safety pin סיכת ביטחון *sikat bitakhon*
sailboat סירת מפרש *sirat mifras*
sale n; (bargains) במבצע
   bemivtza
same אותו דבר *oto davar*
sand חול *khol*
sandal סנדל *sandal*
sanitary napkin תחבושת היגיינית
   takhboshet higiyenit
sapphire ספיר *sapir*
satin סטן *saten*
saucepan סיר *sir*
saucer צלוחית *tzlokhit*
sauna סאונה *sa-una*
save v לשמור *lishmor* [guard]; לחסוך *lakhasokh* [money] ; להציל *lehatzil* [lives]
savings account חשבון חיסכון *kheshbon khisakhon*
scarf צעיף *tza-if*
scenery נוף *nof*
scenic route דרך נוף *derekh nof*
school בית ספר *beyt sefer*
scissors מספריים *mispara-im*
scooter קטנוע *katnoa*
Scotland סקוטלנד *Skotland*
screwdriver מברג *mavreg*

sculpture פסל *pesel*
sea ים *yam*
season עונה *ona*
seat מושב *moshav*
seat belt חגורת בטיחות *khagorat betikhut*
second שניה *shniya*;
   adj נוסף *nosaf*
second class סוג ב' *sug bet*
second-hand shop חנות יד שניה *khanut yad shniya*
section סעיף *sa-if*
see לראות *lirot*
sell למכור *limkor*
send לשלוח *lishloakh*
senior citizen גמלאי / גמלאית *gimla-i (m)* / *gimla-it (f)*
sentence משפט *mishpat*
separated (relationship) פרוד / פרודה *parud (m)* / *pruda (f)*
serious רציני / רצינית *retzini (m)* / *retzinit (f)*
serve (meal) להגיש *lehagish*
service (restaurant) שירות *sherut*
set menu תפריט קבוע *tafrit kavu-a*
sew לתפור *litfor*
shampoo שמפו *shampo*
shape לעצב *le-atzev*
sharp (pain) חד *khad*
shave להתגלח *lehitgale-akh*
shaving brush מברשת גילוח *mivreshet giluakh*
shaving cream קרם גילוח *krem giluakh*
shelf מדף *madaf*
ship אוניה לשלוח *oniya lishlo-akh*
shirt חולצה *khultza*
shoe נעל *na-al*
shoe store חנות נעליים *khanut na-alayim*
shop חנות *khanut*
shopping קניות *kniyot*
shopping area אזור קניות *ezor kniyot*
shopping centre [BE] מרכז קניות *merkaz kniyot*
shopping mall קניון *kenyon*
short קצר / קצרה *katzar (m)* / *ktzara (f)*

shorts מכנסיים קצרים *mikhnasa-im ktzarim*
short-sighted [BE] קצר ראיה / קצרת ראיה *ktzar re-iya (m)* / *kitzrat re-iya (f)*
shoulder כתף *katef*
shovel את *et*
show הופעה הופיע *hofa-ah lehofi-a*
shower (stall) מקלחת *miklakhat*
shrine מזבח *mizbe-akh*
shut לסגור *lisgor*;
   סגור / סגורה *sagur (m)* / *sgura (f)*
shutter (window) תריס *tris*
side צד *tzad*
sightseeing תיירות *tayarut*
sightseeing tour נסיעת תיירות *nesi-at tayarut*
sign שלט *shelet*
sign (notice) לאותת *le-otet*
signature חתימה *khatima*
silk משי *meshi*
silver כסף *kesef*
silverware כלי כסף *kley kesef*
since מאז *me-az*
sing לשיר *lashir*
single (ticket) בודד *boded*; (unmarried) רווק / רווקה *ravak (m)* / *ravaka (f)*
single room חדר לאחד *kheder le-echad*
size; (clothes); (shoes) גודל *godel*
skate להחליק *lehakhlik*
skating rink רחבת החלקה *rakhavat hakhlaka*
skin עור *or*
skirt חצאית *khatzait*
sky שמיים *shamayim*
sleep לישון *lishon*
sleeping bag שק שינה *sak shena*
sleeping car קרון שינה *karon shena*
sleeping pill גלולת שינה *glulat shena*
sleeve שרוול *sharvul*
slice חתיכה *khatikha*
slide (photo) שקופית *shikufit*
slipper נעל בית *na-al bayit*
slow לאט *le-at*

small קטן / קטנה
katan (m) / ktana (f)

smoke n; v עשן; לעשן ashan; leashen

smoker מעשן / מעשנת
me-ashen (m) / me-ashenet (f)

snack חטיף khatif

snack bar מזנון miznon

sneaker נעל התעמלות na-al hitamlut

snorkeling equipment ציוד שנורקלינג
tziyud snorkeling

snow שלג sheleg

soap סבון sabon

soccer כדורגל kaduregel

soccer match משחק כדורגל
miskhak kaduregel

sock גרב gerev

socket (electric) תושבת toshevet

soft רך / רכה rakh (m) / raka (f)

sold out אזל מהמלאי azal mehamelay

someone מישהו / מישהי
mishehu (m) / mishehi (f)

something משהו mashehu

song שיר shir

soon בקרוב bekarov

sore (painful) כואב ko-ev

sore throat כאב גרון ke-ev Garon

sorry סליחה slikha

sort (kind) מעין me-eyn

south דרום darom

souvenir מזכרת mazkeret

souvenir shop חנות מזכרות khanut mazkarot

spa ספא spa

spatula מרית marit

speak v לדבר ledaber

special מיוחד / מיוחדת
meyukhad (m) / meyukhedet (f)

specialist מומחה mumkhe

speciality התמחות hitmakhut

spell v לאיית le-ayet

spend לבזבז levazbez

spine עמוד שדרה amud shidra

sponge ספוג sfog

spoon כף kaf

sport ספורט sport

sporting goods store

חנות מוצרי ספורט khanut mutzrey sport

sprained נקוע / נקועה
naku-a (m) / neku-a (f)

square (shape) מרובע meruba

stadium איצטדיון itztadyon

staff סגל segel

stain כתם ketem

stainless steel פלדת אל חלד pladat al kheled

stairs מדרגות
madregot

stamp n (postage); v (ticket)
בול להחתים
bul lehakhtim

staple לשדך leshadekh

star כוכב kokhav

start v; להתחיל; התחלה
lehatkhil; hatkhala

starter [BE] (meal) מנה ראשונה
mana rishona

station (train); (subway)
תחנה takhana

stationery store חנות למכשירי כתיבה
khanut lemakhshirey ktiva

stay (trip) שהות shahut;
v (remain) להישאר lehisha-er;
v (reside) לגור lagur

steal לגנוב lignov

sterling silver כסף סטרלינג
kesef sterling

sting n; v עוקץ לעקוץ oketz la-akotz

stockings גרביונים
garbiyonim

stomach קיבה keva

stomachache כאב בטן ke-ev beten

stop (bus); v stop תחנה לעצור
takhana la-atzor

store (shop) חנות khanut

store directory מדריך חנויות
madrikh khanuyot

stove תנור tanur

straight ahead ישר yashar

strange מוזר muzar

street רחוב rehov

street map מפת רחובות mapat rehovot

string חוט khut

stroller עגלת ילדים *eglat yeladim*
strong חזק / חזקה *khazak (m) / khazaka (f)*
student סטודנט / סטודנטית *student (m) / studentit (f)*
study v ללמוד *lilmod*
stunning מהמם *mehamem*
sturdy בנוי היטב *banuy heytev*
subway רכבת תחתית *rakevet takhtit*
subway map מפת רכבת תחתית *mapat rakevet takhtit*
suit (man's); (woman's) חליפה *khalifa*
suitcase מזוודה *mizvada*
sun שמש *shemesh*
sunburn כוויה *kviya*
sunglasses משקפי שמש *mishkefey shemesh*
sunstroke מכת שמש *makat shemesh*
sun-tan lotion תחליב שיזוף *takhliv shizuf*
super (gas/ petrol) סופר *super*
supermarket סופרמרקט *supermarket*
supplement n תוסף *tosaf*
suppository פתילה *ptila*
surgery [BE] ניתוח *nitu-akh*
surname שם משפחה *shem mishpakha*
swallow לבלוע *livlo-a*
sweater סודר *sveder*
sweatshirt סווטשירט *svetshert*
sweet מתוק / מתוקה *matok (m) / metuka (f)*
swell להתנפח *lehitnape-akh*
swelling התנפחות *hitnapkhut*
swim v לשחות *liskhot*
swimming שחיה *skhiya*
swimming pool בריכת שחיה *brekhat skhiya*
swimming trunks מכנסי רחצה *mikhnasey rakhatza*
swollen נפוח *nafu-akh*
symbol סמל *semel*
synagogue בית כנסת *beyt Kneset*
synthetic סינתטי *sinteti*
system מערכת *ma-arekhet*

T

table שולחן *shulkhan*
tablet (medical) טבליה *tavlia*
tailor חייט *khayat*
take לקחת *lakakhat*
take away v [BE] לקחת *lakakhat*
taken (occupied) תפוס *tafus*
tampon טמפון *tampon*
tap (water) ברז *terez*
tax מס *mas*
taxi מונית *monit*
taxi rank [BE] תחנת מוניות *takhanat moniyot*
taxi stand תחנת מוניות *takhanat moniyot*
team צוות *tzevet*
tear v לקרוע *likro-a*
teaspoon כפית *kapit*
telephone booth תא טלפון *ta Telefon*
telephone directory מדריך טלפונים *madrikh Telefonim*
telephone n; v טלפון / לטלפן *telefon letalpen*
telephone number מספר טלפון *mispar telefon*
tell לומר *lomar*
temperature טמפרטורה *temperatura*
temple מקדש *mikdash*
temporary זמני *zmani*
tennis court מגרש טניס *migrash tenis*
tennis match משחק טניס *miskhak tenis*
tennis racket מחבט טניס *makhvet tenis*
tent אוהל *ohel*
tent peg יתד אוהל *yated ohel*
tent pole מוט אוהל *mot ohel*
terminal טרמינל, מסוף *terminal, masof*
terrace טרסה *terasa*
terrible נורא *nora*
terrifying מפחיד *mafkhid*
thank להודות *lehodot*
thank you תודה *toda*
theater תיאטרון *te-atron*
theft גניבה *gneva*
then אז *az*
there שם *sham*

thermometer מדחום *madkhom*

thief גנב *ganav*

thigh ירך *yarekh*

thin רזה / רזה *raze (m) / raza (f)*

think (believe) חושב/חושבת *khoshev (m) / khoshevet (f)*

thirsty צמא / צמאה *tzame (m) / tzme-a (f)*

thread חוט *khut*

throat גרון *garon*

through דרך *derekh*

thumb אגודל *agudal*

thunder רעם *ra-am*

thunderstorm סופת רעמים *sufat re-amim*

ticket כרטיס *kartis*

ticket office משרד כרטיסים *misrad kartisim*

tide גאות *ge-ut*

tie v לקשור *likshor*; n עניבה *aniva*

tie clip הביגע תכיס *sikat aniva*

time n ; (recurrent occasion) מועד *mo-ed*

timetable [BE] לוח זמנים *lu-akh zmanim*

tin [BE] (container) קופסת שימורים *kufsat shimurim*

tin opener [BE] פותחן שימורים *potkhan shimurim*

tire צמיג *tzamig*

tired עייף / עייפה *ayef (m) / ayefa (f)*

tissue ניר ממחטת *mimkhetet neyar*

to אל *el*

tobacco טבק *tabak*

tobacconist בעל חנות טבק *ba-al khanut tabak*

today היום *hayom*

toe בוהן *bohen*

toilet [BE] שירותים *herutim*

toilet paper ניר טואלט *neyar to-alet*

toiletry תמרוקים *amrukim*

tomb קבר *kever*

tomorrow מחר *makhar*

tongue לשון *lashon*

tonight הלילה *halayla*

too (also) גם *gam*

too much מדי יותר *yoter miday*

tool כלי *kli*

tooth שן *shen*

toothache כאב שיניים *ke-ev shinayim*

toothbrush מברשת שיניים *mivreshet shinayim*

toothpaste משחת שיניים *mishkhat shinayim*

Torah תורה *torah*

torn (clothes) קרוע *karu-a*

touch v לנגת *laga-at*

tour סיול *tiyul*

tourist office משרד תיירות *misrad tayarut*

tow truck גרר *grar*

towards לכיוון *lekivun*

towel מגבת *magevet*

tower מגדל *migdal*

town עיירה *ayara*

town hall בית העירייה *beyt ha-irya*

toy עוצעצ *tza-atzu-a*

toy store חנות צעצועים *khanut tza-atzu-im*

track (train) מסילה *mesila*

traffic light רמזור *ramzor*

trail שביל *shvil*

trailer טריילר *treyler*; נגרר *nigrar*

train רכבת *rakevet*

tram רכבת קלה *Rakevet kala*

tranquillizer חומר מרגיע *khomer margi-a*

transfer (money) העברה *ha-avara*

translate לתרגם *letargem*

travel לנסוע *linso-a*

travel agency סוכנות נסיעות *sokhnut nesi-ot*

travel guide מדריך טיולים / מדריכת טיולים *madrikh tiyulim (m) / madrikhat tiyulim (f)*

travel sickness מחלת נסיעה *makhalat nesi-a*

traveler's check המחאת נוסעים *hamkha-at nosim*

treatment טיפול *tipul*

tree עץ *etz*

trim לגזום *ligzom*

trip נסיעה *nesi-a*

trolley חשמלית *khasmalit*

trousers [BE] מכנסיים *mikhnasa-im*

T-shirt חולצת טריקו *khultzat triko*

tube שפופרת *shfoferet*
turn (change direction) לפנות *lifnot*
turtleneck צוארון גולף *tzavaron golf*
TV טלביזיה *televizya*
tweezers פינצטה *pintzeta*

U

ugly מכוער *mekho-ar*
umbrella מטריה *mitriya;*
(beach) שימשיה *shimshiya*
unconscious
מחוסר הכרה / מחוסרת הכרה *mekhusar hakara*
(m) / *mekhuseret hakara* (f)
under מתחת *mitakhat*
underground station [BE]
תחנת רכבת תחתית
takhanat rakevet takhtit
underpants תחתונים *takhtonim*
undershirt גופיה *gufiya*
understand להבין *lehavin*
undress להתפשט *lehitpashet*
United States ארצות הברית *srtzot habrit*
university אוניברסיטה *universita*
unleaded (fuel) נטול עופרת
netul oferet
until עד *ad*
up למעלה *lemala*
upstairs בקומה למעלה
bakoma lemala
urgent דחוף *dakhuf*
use להשתמש *lehishtamesh*
usually בדרך כלל
bederekh klal

V

vacancy חדר פנוי
kheder panuy
vacant פנוי *panuy*
vacation חופשה *khufsha*
vaccinate לחסן
lekhasen
vacuum cleaner שואב אבק
shoev avak

valley עמק *emek*
value ערך *erekh*
value-added tax [BE]
מס ערך מוסף
mas erekh musaf
vegetarian
צמחוני / צמחונית
tzimkhoni (m) / *tzimkhonit* (f)
vein וריד *vrid*
very מאוד *meod*
veterinarian וטרינר / וטרינרית *veterinar* (m) /
veterinarit (f)
video camera מצלמת וידיאו *matzlemat video*
view (panorama) נוף *nof*
village כפר *kfar*
visit ביקור n *bikur;*
לבקר v *levaker*
visiting hours שעות ביקור
shot bikur
visually impaired לקויי ראיה
lekuyey re-iya
V-neck מחשוף וי *makhsof vi*
volleyball game
משחק כדור עף
mishkhak kadur af
voltage וולטז' *voltazh*
vomit v להקיא *lehaki*

W

wait v לחכות *lehakot*
waiter מלצר *meltzar*
waiting room חדר המתנה
kheder hamtana
waitress מלצרית
meltzarit
wake להתעורר *lehitorer*
wake-up call שיחת השכמה
sikhat hashkama
Wales וויל ס *wels*
walk הליכה n *halikha*
wall קיר *kir*
wallet ארנק *arnak*
want לרצות *lirtzot*
warm (temperature) חמים *khamim;*
v (reheat) לחמם *lekhamem*

wash לרחוץ *lirkhotz*
washing machine מכונת כביסה *mekhonat kvisa*
watch *n* שעון *sha-on*
water מים *mayim*
waterfall מפל *mapal*
waterproof (clothing)
עמיד במים *me-il geshem*
(literally) מעיל גשם
amid bemayim
water-ski סקי מים
ski mayim
wave *n* גל *gal*
way דרך *derekh*
weather מזג אוויר
mezeg avir
weather forecast
תחזית מזג אוויר
takhazit mezeg avir
week שבוע *shavu-a*
weekend סופשבוע
sofshavu-a
well באר *be-er*
west מערב *ma-arav*
what מה *ma*
wheel גלגל *galgal*
wheelchair כסא גלגלים
kise galgalim
when מתי *matay*
where איפה *eyfo*
which איזה *eyze*
white לבן *lavan*
who מי *mi*
whole שלם *shalem*
why למה *lama*
wide רחב / רחבה
rakhav (m) / rekhava (f)
widow (f) אלמנה *almana;*
(m) אלמן *alman*
wife אישה *isha*
WiFi Wifi *Wi-Fi*
wind רוח *ru-akh*
window; (shop) חלון ראווה
khalon ra-ava
window seat מושב חלון
moshav khalon

windsurfer גלישת רוח
glishat ru-akh
wine list רשימת יינות
reshimat yeynot
wireless אלחוטי *alkhuti*
wish *v* לאכל *le-akhel*
with עם *im*
withdraw (banking) למשוך
limshokh
without ללא *lelo*
woman אישה *isha*
wonderful נהדר / נהדרת
nehedar (m) / nehederet (f)
wood עץ *etz*
wool צמר *tzemer*
word מילה *mila*
work *v* לעבוד *la-avod*
worse גרוע יותר
garu-a yoter
wound פצע *petza*
write לכתוב *likhtov*
wrong לא נכון *lo nakhon*

X

X-ray רנטגן *rentgen*

Y

yacht יאכטה *yakhta*
year שנה *shana*
yellow צהוב *tzahov*
yes כן *ken*
yesterday אתמול *etmol*
yet עדיין *adayin*
young צעיר / צעירה
tza-ir (m) / tze-ira (f)
youth hostel אכסניית נוער
akhsaniyat no-ar

Z

zero אפס *efes*
zip(per) רוכסן *rukhsan*
zoo גן חיות *gan khayot*
zucchini קישוא *kishu*

INDEX

Berlitz pocket guide

ISRAEL

First edition 2019

Editor: Tom Fleming
Author: Simon Griver
Head of DTP and Pre-Press: Rebeka Davies
Managing Editor: Carine Tracanelli
Picture Editor: Tom Smyth
Cartography Update: Carte
Photography Credits: Alamy 22; AWL
Images. 28; Getty Images 26, 92;
Government Press Office 25; iStock 4MC,
4ML, 4TL, 5T, 5TC, 5MC, 5M, 5MC, 5M, 6L,
6R, 7, 7R, 11, 12, 14, 15, 19, 20, 30, 35, 39,
49, 52, 54, 57, 63, 64, 67, 68, 70, 73, 78, 84,
87, 88, 103, 104; Shutterstock 1, 4TC, 16, 33,
36, 41, 42, 44, 46, 51, 58, 61, 74, 77, 81, 83,
91, 97, 99, 100
Cover Picture: AWL Images

Distribution
UK, Ireland and Europe: Apa Publications
(UK) Ltd; sales@insightguides.com
United States and Canada: Ingram
Publisher Services; ips@ingramcontent.com
Australia and New Zealand: Woodslane;
info@woodslane.com.au
Southeast Asia: Apa Publications (SN) Pte;
singaporeoffice@insightguides.com
Worldwide: Apa Publications (UK) Ltd;
sales@insightguides.com

**Special Sales, Content Licensing
and CoPublishing**
Insight Guides can be purchased in bulk
quantities at discounted prices. We can
create special editions, personalised jackets
and corporate imprints tailored to your
needs. sales@insightguides.com;
www.insightguides.biz

Contact us
Every effort has been made to provide
accurate information in this publication,
but changes are inevitable. The publisher
cannot be responsible for any resulting loss,
inconvenience or injury. We would appreciate
it if readers would call our attention to any
errors or outdated information. We also
welcome your suggestions; please contact
us at: berlitz@apaguide.co.uk
www.insightguides.com/berlitz

Berlitz®

speaking your language

phrase book & dictionary
phrase book & CD

Available in: Arabic, Brazilian Portuguese*, Burmese*, Cantonese
Chinese, Croatian, Czech*, Danish*, Dutch, English, Filipino, Finnish*, French,
German, Greek, Hebrew*, Hindi*, Hungarian*, Indonesian, Italian, Japanese,
Korean, Latin American Spanish, Malay, Mandarin Chinese, Mexican Spanish,
Norwegian, Polish, Portuguese, Romanian*, Russian, Spanish, Swedish, Thai,
Turkish, Vietnamese
*Book only